Cleveland Indians 2019

A Baseball Companion

Edited by Patrick Dubuque, Aaron Gleeman and Bret Sayre

Baseball Prospectus

Craig Brown and Dave Pease, Consultant Editors
Rob McQuown and Harry Pavlidis, Statistics Editors

Copyright © 2019 by DIY Baseball, LLC.
All rights reserved

This book or any part thereof may not be reproduced or transmitted in any form or by any means, electronic or mechanical, including photocopying, recording, or by any information storage and retrieval system, without permission in writing from the publisher.

Limit of Liability/Disclaimer of Warranty: While the publisher and the author have used their best efforts in preparing this book, they make no representations or warranties with respect to the accuracy or completeness of the contents of this book and specifically disclaim any implied warranties of merchantability or fitness for a particular purpose. No warranty may be created or extended by sales representatives or written sales materials. The advice and strategies contained herein may not be suitable for your situation. You should consult with a professional where appropriate. Neither the publisher nor the author shall be liable for any loss of profit or any other commercial damages, including but not limited to special, incidental, consequential, or other damages.

Library of Congress Cataloging-in-Publication Data:
paperback
ISBN-13: 978-1-949332-06-3

Project Credits
Cover Design: Kathleen Dyson
Interior Design and Production: Jeff Pease, Dave Pease
Layout: Jeff Pease, Dave Pease

Baseball icon courtesy of Uberux, from https://www.shareicon.net/author/uberux

Ballpark diagram courtesy of Lou Spirito/THIRTY81 Project, https://thirty81project.com/

Manufactured in the United States of America
10 9 8 7 6 5 4 3 2 1

Table of Contents

Foreword v
    Rob Mains

Statistical Introduction vii

Part 1: Team Analysis

Table for Two: Previewing the 2019 Cleveland Indians 3
    Zach Crizer and Rob Silver

Performance Graphs 9

2018 Team Performance 10

2019 Team Projections 11

Team Personnel 12

Progressive Field Stats 13

Indians Team Analysis 15

Part 2: Player Analysis

Indians Player Analysis 22

Indians Prospects 99

Part 3: Featured Articles

The Hole in The Shift is Fixing Itself 113
    Russell Carleton

The State of the Quality Start 117
    Rob Mains

Heads-Up Hacking—The First Pitch 123
    Matthew Trueblood

A Hymn for the Index Stat 129
    Patrick Dubuque

Index of Names 133

Foreword

Rob Mains

Welcome to this companion of the 2019 Cleveland Indians. We at Baseball Prospectus are excited to provide this analysis of the Indians.

Our website, Baseball Prospectus, is a leader in delivering high-quality commentary and data to baseball fans everywhere. To some, those words—commentary and data—appear mutually exclusive. There are people out there who believe that traditional analysis and advanced analytics must run on different paths. But the simplistic narrative of stats vs. traditionalists just isn't true. Every team's analytics department interacts with scouting, development, and major league operations with a common goal: Delivering a championship. New technologies, like radar tracking of pitch speeds and movement, enable talent evaluators to focus on qualitative aspects of pitching like mechanics and pitch sequencing. In-game strategies like infield shifts, based on batters' hit tendencies, help turn balls in play into outs. Hitters use information to adjust their swings to maximize run production.

All these numbers can seem, at best, intimidating, and at worst, counterproductive to the casual fan. Even as technology and analysis have embedded themselves deeply into the way teams run, it can often feel like statistics create a displacement between the viewer and the sport, breaking them out of the action. And yet every fan incorporates the numbers to some degree; stats like batting average and earned run average, so fundamental to how we talk about performance, are actually complicated formulas. They don't bother people because those formulas have become second nature, as easy to translate as the action on the field.

Along the way, new statistics have entered baseball's lexicon. You'll see some of them, like on-base percentage (which measures a batter's ability to get on base via walk, hit batter, or hit), OPS (on-base plus slugging), and average exit velocity (the speed of balls off a hitter's bat) on broadcasts. Others, like DRC+, might well be new to you. Some of them have been well-defined to the public, others haven't. That lack of context has created ambiguity. Fans know that a ball hit 100 mph is scorched, but does that mean extra bases? (Not if it's hit on the ground or high in the air it doesn't.)

For those who are amenable to them, the new statistics can increase the enjoyment and understanding of the game. They can help fans identify when a pitcher is tiring, when a stolen base or a bunt attempt makes sense (and, more often, when it doesn't), or how a team's lineup might be constructed. Websites like Baseball Prospectus add to that understanding by weaving metrics into the narrative of the game. That's the goal of this publication: to take some of the newer, more complicated statistics and make them as intuitive as the ones on the back of old baseball cards.

But you don't need to love analytics to love baseball. The fans at BP who worked together to write this guide are captivated first and foremost by the game itself. We're drawn to Aaron Judge's power, Francisco Lindor's glove, Billy Hamilton's speed and Patrick Corbin's slider and don't need numbers to tell us why they're so mesmerizing. The underlying statistics provide depth to the game that we all love.

We hope you'll find that this guide helps you better understand the Indians. Our analysts have studied the team's major league personnel and its minor league affiliates to identify their strengths and weaknesses, both the obvious ones and those that only a careful dissection of players' performances—yes, including the data—can reveal. You don't need us to tell you who was good and who wasn't in 2018, but our models and writers can help you project how each player is going to perform this year and beyond, and appreciate the greatness of each new game as it unfolds. As in the sport itself, the human and analytic components combine to generate a deeper overall understanding.

Think back to the first time you saw a baseball game on a high-definition TV. You'd grown familiar with how the game looked and felt on a picture tube. But new TV allowed you to see details that you'd never seen before. That's how advanced statistics work. The game itself is why you're here and why you're buying this. (And, for that matter, why we wrote it.) The statistical measures provide the sharper focus, the detail, the depth of knowledge that you didn't have before, generating an overall superior picture. Enjoy the view.

—*Rob Mains is an author of Baseball Prospectus.*

Statistical Introduction

Sports are, fundamentally, a blend of athletic endeavor and storytelling. Baseball, like any other sport, tells its stories in so many ways: in the arc of a game from the stands or a season from the box scores, in photos, or even in numbers. At Baseball Prospectus, we understand that statistics don't replace observation or any of baseball's stories, but complement everything else that makes the game so much fun.

What stats help us with is with patterns and precision, variance and value. This book can help you learn things you may not see from watching a game or hundred, whether it's the path of a career over time or the breadth of the entire MLB. We'd also never ask you to choose between our numbers and the experience of viewing a game from the cheap seats or the comfort of your home; our publication combines running the numbers with observations and wisdom from some of the brightest minds we can find. But if you *do* want to learn more about the numbers beyond what's on the backs of player jerseys, let us help explain.

Offense

At the end of this past year, we've revised our methodology for determining batting value. Long-time readers of Baseball Prospectus will notice that we've retired True Average in favor of a new metric: Deserved Runs Created Plus (DRC+). Developed by Jonathan Judge and our stats team, this statistic measures everything a player does at the plate–reaching base, hitting for power, making outs, and moving runners over–and puts it on a scale where 100 equals league-average performance. A DRC+ of 150 is terrific, a DRC+ of 100 is average, and a DRC+ of 75 means you better be an excellent defender.

DRC+ also does a better job than any of our previous metrics in taking contextual factors into account. The model adjusts for how the park affects performance, but also for things like the talent of the opposing pitcher, value of different types of batted-ball events, league, temperature, and other factors. It's able to describe a player's expected offensive contribution than any other statistic we've found over the years, and also does a better job of predicting future performance as well.

The other aspect of run-scoring is baserunning, which we quantify using Baserunning Runs. BRR not only records the value of stolen bases (or getting caught in the act), but also accounts for a runner's ability to go first to third on a single or advance on a fly ball.

Defense

Where offensive value is *relatively* easy to identify and understand, defensive value is ... not. Over the past dozen years, the sabermetric community has focused mostly on stats based on zone data: a real-live human person records the type of batted ball and estimated landing location, and models are created that give expected outs. From there, you can compare fielders' actual outs to those expected ones. Simple, right?

Unfortunately, zone data has two major issues. First, zone data is recorded by commercial data providers who keep the raw data private unless you pay for it. (All the statistics we build in this book and on our website use public data as inputs.) That hurts our ability to test assumptions or duplicate results. Second, over the years it has become apparent that there's quite a bit of "noise" in zone-based fielding analysis. Sometimes the conclusions drawn from zone data don't hold up to scrutiny, and sometimes the different data provided by different providers don't look anything alike, giving wildly different results. Sometimes the hard-working professional stringers or scorers might unknowingly inflict unconscious bias into the mix: for example good fielders will often be credited with more expected outs despite the data, and ballparks with high press boxes tend to score more line drives than ones with a lower press box.

Enter our Fielding Runs Above Average (FRAA). For most positions, FRAA is built from play-by-play data, which allows us to avoid the subjectivity found in many other fielding metrics. The idea is this: count how many fielding plays are made by a given player and compare that to expected plays for an average fielder at their position (based on pitcher ground-ball tendencies and batter handedness). Then we adjust for park and base-out situations.

When it comes to catchers, our methodology is a little different thanks to the laundry list of responsibilities they're tasked with beyond just, well, catching and throwing the ball. By now you've probably heard about "framing" or the art of making umpires more likely to call balls outside the strike zone for strikes. To put this into one tidy number, we incorporate pitch tracking data (for the years it exists) and adjust for important factors like pitcher, umpire, batter, and home-field advantage using a mixed-model approach. This grants us a number for how many strikes the catcher is personally adding to (or subtracting from) his pitchers' performance ... which we then convert to runs added or lost using linear weights.

Framing is one of the biggest parts of determining catcher value, but we also take into account blocking balls from going past, whether a scorer deems it a passed ball or a wild pitch. We use a similar approach–one that really benefits from the pitch tracking data that tells us what ends up in the dirt and what doesn't. We also include a catcher's ability to prevent stolen bases and how well they field balls in play, and *finally* we come up with our FRAA for catchers.

Pitching

Both pitching and fielding make up the half of baseball that isn't run scoring: run prevention. Separating pitching from fielding is a tough task, and most recent pitching analysis has branched off from Voros McCracken's famous (and controversial) statement, "There is little if any difference among major-league pitchers in their ability to prevent hits on balls hit in the field of play." The research of the analytic community has validated this to some extent, and there are a host of "defense-independent" pitching measures that have been developed to try and extricate the effect of the defense behind a hurler from the pitcher's work.

Our solution to this quandry is Deserved Run Average (DRA), our core pitching metric. DRA looks like earned run average (ERA), the tried-and-true pitching stat you've seen on every baseball broadcast or box score from the past century, but it's very different. To start, DRA takes an event-by-event look at what the pitchers does, and adjusts the value of that event based on different environmental factors like park, batter, catcher, umpire, base-out situation, run differential, inning, defense, home field advantage, pitcher role, and temperature. That mixed model gives us a pitcher's expected contribution, similar to what we do for our DRC+ model for hitters and FRAA model for catchers. (Oh, and we also consider the pitcher's effect on basestealing and on balls getting past the catcher.)

It's important to note that DRA is set to the scale of runs allowed per nine innings (RA9) instead of ERA, which makes DRA's scale slightly higher than ERA's. The reason for this is because ERA tends to overrate three types of pitchers:

1. Pitchers who play in parks where scorers hand out more errors. Official scorers differ significantly in the frequency at which they assign errors to fielders.
2. Ground-ball pitchers, because a substantial proportion of errors occur on grounders.
3. Pitchers who aren't very good. Better pitchers often allow fewer unearned runs than bad pitchers, because good pitchers tend to find ways to get out of jams.

Since the last time you picked up an edition of this book, we've also made a few minor changes to DRA to make it better. Recent research into "tunneling"–the act of throwing consecutive pitches that appear similar from a batter's point of view until after the swing decision point–data has given us a new contextual factor to account for in DRA: plate distance. This refers to the distance between successive pitches as they approach the plate, and while it has a smaller effect than factors like velocity or whiff rate, it still can help explain pitcher strikeout rate in our model.

New Pitching Metrics for 2019

We're including a few "new" pitching metrics for 2019's suite of Baseball Prospectus publications, but you may be familiar with them if you've spent time scouring the internet for stats.

Fastball Percentage

Our fastball percentage (FB%) statistic measures how frequently a pitcher throws a pitch classified as a "fastball," measured as a percentage of overall pitches thrown. We qualify three types of fastballs:

1. The traditional four-seam fastball;
2. The two-seam fastball or sinker;
3. "Hard cutters," which are pitches that have the movement profile of a cut fastball and are used as the pitcher's primary offering or in place of a more traditional fastball.

For example, a pitcher with a FB% of 67 throws any combination of these three pitches about two-thirds of the time.

Whiff Rate

Everybody loves a swing and a miss, and whiff rate (WHF) measures how frequently pitchers induce a swinging strike. To calculate WHF, we add up all the pitches thrown that ended with a swinging strike, then divide that number by a pitcher's total pitches thrown. Most often, high whiff rates correlate with high strikeout rates (and overall effective pitcher performance).

Called Strike Probability

Called Strike Probability (CSP) is a number that represents the likelihood that all of a pitcher's pitches will be called a strike while controlling for location, pitcher and batter handedness, umpire and count. Here's how it works: on each pitch, our model determines how many times (out of 100) that a similar pitch was called for a strike given those factors mentioned above, and when normalized for each batter's strike zone. Then we average the CSP for all pitches thrown by a pitcher in a season, and that gives us the yearly CSP percentage you see in the stats boxes.

As you might imagine, pitchers with a higher CSP are more likely to work in the zone, where pitchers with a lower CSP are likely locating their pitches outside the normal strike zone, for better or for worse.

Projections

Many of you aren't turning to this book just for a look at what a player has done, but for a look at what a player is going to do: the PECOTA projections. PECOTA, initially developed by Nate Silver (who has moved on to greater fame as a political analyst), consists of three parts:

1. Major-league equivalencies, which use minor-league statistics to project how a player will perform in the major leagues;
2. Baseline forecasts, which use weighted averages and regression to the mean to estimate a player's current true talent level; and
3. Aging curves, which uses the career paths of comparable players to estimate how a player's statistics are likely to change over time.

With all those important things covered, let's take a look at what's in the book this year.

Team Prospectus

You bought this book to learn more about your favorite (or maybe least-favorite, who are we to judge?) team, so let's talk about them. After a thoughtful preview of the 2019 season, you'll be presented with our Team Prospectus. This outlines many of the key statistics for each team's 2018 season, as well as a very inviting stadium diagram.

First you'll find the Performance Graphs page. The first is the 2018 Hit List Ranking. This shows our Hit List Rank for the team on each day of the 2018 season and is intended to give you a picture of the ups and downs of the team's season, including their highest and lowest ranks of the year. Hit List Rank measures overall team performance and drives the Hit List Power Rankings at the baseballprospectus.com website.

The second graph is Committed Payroll and helps you see how the team's payroll has compared to the MLB and divisional average payrolls over time. Payroll figures are currents as of January 1, 2019; with so many free agents still unsigned as of this writing, the final 2018 figure will likely be significantly different for many teams. (In the meantime, you can always find the most current data at Baseball Prospectus' Cot's Baseball Contracts page.)

Cleveland Indians 2019

The third graph is Farm System Ranking and displays how the Baseball Prospectus prospect team has ranked the organization's farm system since 2007. It also indicates the highest and lowest ranks that the farm system achieved over that time.

We start the Team Performance page with the squad's unadjusted and third-order 2018 win-loss records, presented in divisional context. We then list the three highest performing hitters and pitchers by WARP for 2018. Beneath that are a host of other team statistics. **Pythag** presents an adjusted 2018 winning percentage, calculated by taking runs scored per game (**RS/G**) and runs allowed per game (**RA/G**) for the team, and running them through a version of Bill James' Pythagorean formula that was refined and improved by David Smyth and Brandon Heipp. (The formula is called "Pythagenpat," which is equally fun to type and to say.)

Next up is **DRC+**, described earlier, to indicate the overall hitting ability of the team either above or below league-average. Run prevention on the pitching side is covered by **DRA** (also mentioned earlier) and another metric: Fielding Independent Pitching (**FIP**), which calculates another ERA-like statistic based on strikeouts, walks, and home runs recorded. Defensive Efficiency Rating (**DER**) tells us the percentage of balls in play turned into outs for the team, and is a quick fielding shorthand that rounds out run prevention.

After that, we have several measures related to roster composition, as opposed to on-field performance. **B-Age** and **P-Age** tell us the average age of a team's batters and pitchers, respectively. **Salary** is the combined team payroll for all on-field players, and Doug Pappas' Marginal Dollars per Marginal Win (**M$/MW**) tells us how much money a team spent to earn production above replacement level.

Ending this batch of statistics is the number of disabled list days a team had over the season (**DL Days**) and the amount of salary paid to players on the disabled list (**$ on DL**); this final number is expressed as a percentage of total payroll.

Next to each of these stats, we've listed each team's MLB rank in that category from 1st to 30th. In this, 1st always indicates a positive outcome and 30th a negative outcome, except in the case of salary–1st is highest.

The Team Projections page is intended to convey the team's operational capacity entering the 2019 season. We start with the team's PECOTA projected record for 2019, again in divisional context. The **+/-** column indicates how many more or less wins the team is projected to get than they got in 2018. We then list the three highest projected hitters and pitchers by WARP for 2018. A brief farm system summary follows, with the team's top prospect and number of BP Top 101 Prospects. Finally, we list the key new players and departed players, along with their 2019 projected WARP.

Alex Bregman 3B

Born: 03/30/94 Age: 25 Bats: R Throws: R
Height: 6'0" Weight: 180 Origin: Round 1, 2015 Draft (#2 overall)

YEAR	TEAM	LVL	AGE	PA	R	2B	3B	HR	RBI	BB	K	SB	CS	AVG/OBP/SLG
2016	CCH	AA	22	285	54	16	2	14	46	42	26	5	3	.297/.415/.559
2016	FRE	AAA	22	83	17	6	0	6	15	5	12	2	1	.333/.373/.641
2016	HOU	MLB	22	217	31	13	3	8	34	15	52	2	0	.264/.313/.478
2017	HOU	MLB	23	626	88	39	5	19	71	55	97	17	5	.284/.352/.475
2018	HOU	MLB	24	705	105	51	1	31	103	96	85	10	4	.286/.394/.532
2019	HOU	MLB	25	675	96	38	3	23	78	73	107	12	4	.272/.359/.463

Breakout: 6%   Improve: 52%   Collapse: 5%   Attrition: 2%   MLB: 100%
Comparables: Anthony Rendon, David Wright, Pablo Sandoval

YEAR	TEAM	LVL	AGE	PA	DRC+	VORP	BABIP	BRR	FRAA	WARP
2016	CCH	AA	22	285	172	38.9	.286	1.6	SS(51): -3.4, 3B(11): 1.4	2.7
2016	FRE	AAA	22	83	161	10.0	.333	-1.2	SS(14): 2.1, LF(3): -0.1	0.8
2016	HOU	MLB	22	217	107	9.6	.317	0.5	3B(40): 0.9, SS(6): -0.1	1.1
2017	HOU	MLB	23	626	114	34.7	.311	-1.5	3B(132): 8.7, SS(30): -2.9	3.9
2018	HOU	MLB	24	705	150	72.6	.289	-1.6	3B(136): 5.4, SS(28): -0.4	7.4
2019	HOU	MLB	25	675	125	37.3	.295	0.0	3B 7, SS 0	4.6

After the projections page, we share a few items about the team's home ballpark. There's the aforementioned diagram of the park's dimensions (including distances to the outfield wall), a few important biographical facts about the stadium, a graphic showing the height of the wall from the left-field pole to the right-field pole, and a table showing three-year park factors for the stadium. The park factors are displayed as indexes where 100 is average, 110 means that the park inflates the statistic in question by 10 percent, and 90 means that the park deflates the statistic in question by 10 percent.

Following the ballpark page, we have a **Personnel** section that lists many of the important decision-makers and upper-level field and operations staff members for the franchise, as well as any former Baseball Prospectus staff members who are currently part of the organization.

Position Players

After all that information and a thoughtful bylined essay covering each team, we present our player comments. Each player is listed with the major-league team who employed him as of early January 2019. If a player changed teams after that point via free agency, trade, or any other method, you'll be able to find them in the book for their previous squad.

First, we cover biographical information (age is as of June 30, 2019) before moving onto the stats themselves. Our statistic columns include standard identifying information like **YEAR**, **TEAM**, **LVL** (level of affiliated play) and **AGE** before getting into the numbers. Next, we provide raw, unstranslated numbers like you might find on the back of your dad's baseball cards: **PA** (plate appearances), **R** (runs), **2B** (doubles), **3B** (triples), **HR** (home runs), **RBI** (runs batted in), **BB** (walks), **K** (strikeouts), **SB** (stolen bases) and **CS** (caught stealing). Then we have unadjusted "slash" statistics: **AVG** (batting average), **OBP** (on-base percentage) and **SLG** (slugging percentage).

Just below the stats box is **PECOTA** data, which is discussed further in a following section. After that, it's on to a pithy and always-informative comment written by a member of the Baseball Prospectus staff, before we cover more stats.

The second text box repeats YEAR, TEAM, LVL, AGE, and PA, then moves on to **DRC+** (Deserved Runs Created Plus), which we described earlier as total offensive expected contribution compared to the league average. Next, one of our oldest active metrics, **VORP** (Value Over Replacement Player), considers offensive production, position and plate appearances. In essence, it is the number of runs contributed beyond what a replacement-level player at the same position would contribute if given the same percentage of team plate appearances. VORP does not consider the quality of a player's defense.

BABIP (batting average on balls in play) tells us how often a ball in play fell for a hit, and can help us identify whether a batter may have been lucky or not … but note that high BABIPs also tend to follow the great hitters of our time, as well as speedy singles hitters who put the ball on the ground.

The next item is **BRR** (Baserunning Runs), which covers all of a player's baserunning accomplishments which includes (but isn't limited to) swiped bags and failed attempts. Next is **FRAA** (Fielding Runs Above Average), which also includes the number of games previously played at each position noted in parentheses. Multi-position players have only their two most frequent positions listed here, but their total FRAA number reflects all positions played.

Our last column here is **WARP** (Wins Above Replacement Player). WARP estimates the total value of a player, which means for hitters it takes into account hitting runs above average (calculated using the DRC+ model), BRR and FRAA. Then, it makes an adjustment for positions played and gives the player a credit for plate appearances based upon the difference between "replacement level"¬–which is derived from the quality of players added to a team's roster after the start of the season¬–and the league average.

Catchers

Catchers are a special breed, and thus they have earned their own separate box which displays some of the defensive metrics that we've built just for them. As an example, let's check out J.T. Realmuto.

YEAR	TEAM	P. COUNT	FRM RUNS	BLK RUNS	THRW RUNS	TOT RUNS
2016	MIA	18935	-8.5	1.8	2.1	-5.6
2017	MIA	18959	5.3	1.7	1.0	9.1
2018	MIA	16399	-0.4	0.9	0.1	0.4
2019	PHI	18448	-1.4	1.5	0.7	0.8

The **YEAR** and **TEAM** columns match what you'd find in the other stat box. **P. COUNT** indicates the number of pitches thrown while the catcher was behind the plate, including swinging strikes, fouls, and balls in play. **FRM RUNS** is the total run value the catcher provided (or cost) his team by influencing the umpire to call strikes where other catchers did not. **BLK RUNS** expresses the total run value above or below average for the catcher's ability to prevent wild pitches and passed balls. **THRW RUNS** is calculated using a similar model as the previous two statistics, and it measures a catcher's ability to throw out basestealers but also to dissuade them from testing his arm in the first place. It takes into account factors like the pitcher (including his delivery and pickoff move) and baserunner (who could be as fast as Billy Hamilton or as slow as Yonder Alonso). **TOT RUNS** is the sum of all of the previous three statistics.

Pitchers

Let's give our pitchers a turn, using 2018 NL Cy Young winner Jacob deGrom as our example. Take a look at his first stat block: the first line and the **YEAR**, **TEAM**, **LVL** and **AGE** columns are the same as in the position player example earlier.

Here too, we have a series of columns that display raw, unadjusted statistics compiled by the pitcher over the course of a season: **W** (wins), **L** (losses), **SV** (saves), **G** (games pitched), **GS** (games started), **IP** (innings pitched), **H** (hits allowed) and **HR** (home runs allowed). Next we have two statistics that are rates: **BB/9** (walks per nine innings) and **K/9** (strikeouts per nine innings), before returning to the unadjusted **K** (strikeouts).

Next up is **GB%** (ground ball percentage), which is the percentage of all batted balls that were hit in the ground, including both outs and hits. Remember, this is based on observational data and subject to human error, so please approach this with a healthy dose of skepticism.

BABIP (batting average on balls in play) is calculated using the same methodology as it is for position players, but it often tells us more about a pitcher than it does a hitter. With pitchers, a high BABIP is often due to poor defense or bad luck, and can often be an indicator of potential rebound, and a low BABIP may be cause to expect performance regression. (A typical league-average BABIP is close to .290-.300.)

After a witty 150ish words on the player like only Baseball Prospectus's staff can provide, it's on to that second stat block, which repeats the YEAR, TEAM, LVL, and AGE columns. The metrics **WHIP** (walks plus hits per inning pitched) and **ERA**

Cleveland Indians 2019

(earned run average) are old standbys: WHIP measures walks and hits allowed on a per-inning basis, while ERA measures earned runs on a nine-inning basis. Neither of these stats are translated or adjusted.

DRA (Deserved Run Average) was described at length earlier, and measures how many runs the pitcher "deserved" to allow per nine innings. Please note that since we lack all the data points that would make for a "real" DRA for minor-league events, the DRA displayed for minor league partial-seasons is based off of different data. (That data is a modified version of our cFIP metric, which you can find more information about on our website.)

Jacob deGrom RHP
Born: 06/19/88   Age: 31   Bats: L   Throws: R
Height: 6'4"   Weight: 180   Origin: Round 9, 2010 Draft (#272 overall)

YEAR	TEAM	LVL	AGE	W	L	SV	G	GS	IP	H	HR	BB/9	K/9	K	GB%	BABIP
2016	NYN	MLB	28	7	8	0	24	24	148	142	15	2.2	8.7	143	47%	.312
2017	NYN	MLB	29	15	10	0	31	31	201[1]	180	28	2.6	10.7	239	48%	.305
2018	NYN	MLB	30	10	9	0	32	32	217	152	10	1.9	11.2	269	48%	.281
2019	NYN	MLB	31	13	9	0	31	31	186	145	18	2.3	10.7	221	46%	.286

Breakout: 8%   Improve: 29%   Collapse: 28%   Attrition: 6%   MLB: 85%
Comparables: Erik Bedard, A.J. Burnett, CC Sabathia

YEAR	TEAM	LVL	AGE	WHIP	ERA	DRA	WARP	MPH	FB%	WHF	CSP
2016	NYN	MLB	28	1.20	3.04	3.30	3.5	96.3	59.6	12.1	47.2
2017	NYN	MLB	29	1.19	3.53	3.02	5.7	97.2	55.5	14.5	49.5
2018	NYN	MLB	30	0.91	1.70	2.09	8.0	98.2	52.1	16.3	48.4
2019	NYN	MLB	31	1.02	2.91	3.23	3.9	96.6	54.5	14.8	48.2

Just like with hitters, **WARP** (Wins Above Replacement Player) is a total value metric that puts pitchers of all stripes on the same scale as position players. We use DRA as the primary input for our calculation of WARP. You might notice that relief pitchers (due to their limited innings) may have a lower WARP than you were expecting or than you might see in other WARP-like metrics. WARP does not take leverage into account, just the actions a pitcher performs and the expected value of those actions ... which ends up judging high-leverage relief pitchers differently than you might imagine given their prestige and market value.

MPH gives you the pitcher's 95th percentile velocity for the noted season, in order to give you an idea of what the *peak* fastball velocity a pitcher possesses. Since this comes from our pitch tracking data, it is not publicly available for minor-league pitchers.

Finally, we display the three new pitching metrics we described earlier. **FB%** (fastball percentage) gives you the percentage of fastballs thrown out of all pitches. **WhiffRt** (whiff rate) tells you the percentage of swinging strikes induced out of all pitches. **CS Prob** (called strike probability) expresses the likelihood of all pitches thrown to result in a called strike, after controlling for factors like handedness, umpire, pitch type, count, and location.

PECOTA

All players have PECOTA projections for 2019, as well as a set of other numbers that describe the performance of comparable players according to PECOTA. All projections for 2019 are for the player at the date we went to press in early January and are projected into the league and park context as indicated by the team abbreviation. All PECOTA projected statistics represent a player's projected major-league performance.

The numbers beneath the player's stats–Breakout, Improve, Collapse, Attrition–are part and parcel of the PECOTA projections. They estimate the likelihood of changes in performance relative to the player's previously-established level of production, based on the performance of comparable players:

Breakout Rate is the percent change that a player's production will improve by at least 20 percent relative to the weighted average of his performance over his most recent seasons.

Improve Rate is the percent chance that a player's production will improve at all relative to his baseline performance. A player who is expected to perform just the same as he has in the recent past will have an Improve Rate of 50 percent.

Collapse Rate is the percent chance that a position player's production will decline by at least 25 percent relative to his baseline performance.

Attrition Rate operates on playing time rather than performance. Specifically, it measures the likelihood that a player's playing time will decrease by at least 50 percent relative to his established level.

Breakout Rate and Collapse Rate can sometimes be counterintuitive for players who have already experienced a radical change in performance level. It's also worth noting that the projected decline in a player's rate performances might not be indicative of an expected decline in underlying ability or skill, but could just be an anticipated correction following a breakout season.

MLB% is the percentage of similar players who played in the major leagues in their relevant season.

The final pieces of information are the player's three highest-scoring comparable players as determined by PECOTA. All comparables represent a snapshot of how the listed player was performing at the same age as the current player, so if a 23-year-old pitcher is compared to Bartolo Colon, he's actually being compared to a 23-year-old Colon, not the version that pitched for the Rangers in 2018, nor to Colon's career as a whole.

Cleveland Indians 2019

A few points about pitcher projections. First, we aren't yet projecting peak velocity, so that column will be blank in the PECOTA lines. Second, projecting DRA is trickier than evaluating past performance, because it is unclear how deserving each pitcher will be of his anticipated outcomes. However, we know that another DRA-related statistic–contextual FIP or cFIP–estimates future run scoring very well. So for PECOTA, the projected DRA figures you see are based on the past cFIPs generated by the pitcher and comparable players over time, along with the other factors described above.

Lineouts

In each chapter's Lineouts section, you'll find abbreviated text comments, as well as most of same information you'd find in our full player comments. We limit the stats boxes in this section to only including the 2018 information for each player.

Exclusive Player Visualizations

In our constant battle to provide you with new and interesting baseball content you can't find anywhere else, we've added a trio of data visualizations to each hitter's entry in these books and a pair of visualizations for each pitcher.

For hitters, you'll find three new infographics. The first is each player's **Batted Ball Distribution**, which displays the five major sections of the field: LF (left), LCF (left center), CF (center), RCF (right center), and RF (right). The percentage indicated tells us what percentage of batted balls from that hitter fell within that part of the field during the 2018 season. We've also included the hitter's slugging percentage on balls in play (also called **SLGCON**) for that part of the field.

You'll also see two heatmaps: **Strike Zone vs LHP** and **Strike Zone vs RHP**. These heat maps represent a view of the strike zone from behind the catcher. Areas where there is a darker coloration represent the places where a higher percentage of pitches resulted in hits. In other words, the heatmap represents a hitter's "sweet spots" for getting hits against either left-handed or right-handed pitchers, depending on the image.

Pitchers get two images that help explain what their pitches look like from a hitter's perspective: **Pitch Shape vs LHH** and **Pitch Shape vs RHH**. These images show you the shape and the "tunneling" effect of each pitcher's offerings from the batter's perspective. For each type of pitch that a pitcher throws (represented by an indicator shape), there's a set of dots indicating the flight path, where each dot represents a 0.01-second interval. This maps the average trajectory and speed of an offering, ending where the ball crosses the plate. The solid black box represents the regular strike zone, while the gray contour lines indicate the range of locations that a pitcher typically works in.

Below the image, we provide a bit more detailed information about each pitcher's average offering in the **Pitch Types** box. Here, we also list each of the pitcher's major offerings under the **Type** column.

- **Fastballs** (which usually refers to the four-seam variation)
- **Sinkers** and/or two-seam fastballs
- **Cutters** (which could include "hard" cutters like cut fastballs and "soft" cutters that resemble hard sliders)
- **Changeups** (not including most splitters)
- **Splitters** (split-fingered pitches, forkballs, and some split-changes)
- **Sliders** and/or slurves
- **Curveballs** (including spike-curveballs and knuckle-curveballs, as well as some slurvy curves)
- **Slow curveballs** and/or eephus pitches
- **Knuckleballs**
- **Screwballs**

The **Freq** column indicates the percentage of overall pitches that fall into each of those type categories; if a pitcher has a 16.55% score for changeups, then that's the percent of all pitches that he throws as changeups. **Velo** is exactly what you think it is: the average miles per hour for each pitch type. **H Mov** is the number of inches of horizontal movement on the average pitch of that type, while **V Mov** is the number of inches of vertical movement on the average pitch of that type. (At Baseball Prospectus, we measure this over the long flight of the ball and include gravity into the V Mov number in order to give you the most realistic representation of what the pitch *actually* does.)

If you're wondering about the second number in brackets, that's the index for that velocity or movement compared to the league average. Like DRC+, a score of 100 means that the speed or movement is about the same as league average, while a higher score means that there's higher velocity or movement than the league average. Numbers below 100 indicate less velocity or movement than the league average.

Part 1: Team Analysis

Table for Two: Previewing the 2019 Cleveland Indians

Zach Crizer and Rob Silver

How did the Indians approach the offseason, and did they do well given their aims?

ROB SILVER: So I assume the 29 other team previews will have some version of 'boy, what a crazy offseason it's been for our assigned team.' But boy, what a crazy offseason it's been for Cleveland. They have as good a core of players as anyone, so obviously the dominant story was about them trying to shed one—or more—of their top pitchers. While they didn't end up doing that, is there any doubt they're a worse team than the day they got eliminated from the playoffs? What the hell is going on in Cleveland?

ZACH CRIZER: Just… a lot of penny-pinching. To hear them tell it, they're shaking the office couch cushions for spare change or maybe a left fielder. You can do this basic rundown for half their lineup, but I'm going to do it about Jordan Luplow (sorry, Jordan). It's one thing to take a flier on Luplow as a slugging fourth outfielder. It's another to slot him into a quasi-starting role on a rebuilding team. It's an entirely different ballgame to make him one of the three best outfielders on a contender.

And that's the Indians right now; they see they're overwhelming favorites to win the AL Central, so they're not even bothering to better themselves. Right? Is there any other rhyme or reason to this?

ROB: And maybe that makes their approach perfectly rational. They've won the AL Central by 30 combined games the last two years. PECOTA has them winning the division by a rather staggering 16 games this year so why not feature Luplow every day? My God, that's sort of depressing.

Is there a scenario you can see where they don't win the division again this year? How does that happen?

ZACH: The scenario where they are toppled in the division probably involves a test (or tests) of their depth. Francisco Lindor (projected for 5 WARP, possibly the third-best baseball player on Earth right now) is already dealing with an injury that could delay the start of his season. Jose Ramirez (projected for 5.1 WARP) is also a mortal human man with muscles that can be strained. As far as I can tell, they are both backed up by some combination of Max Moroff, Yu-Cheng Chang and Eric Stamets. Taking any of the major cogs out of that lineup could cause a serious breakdown.

Cleveland is really deriving strength from the rotation, though. With Mike Clevinger projected for the *worst* ERA in the bunch at 3.87, this is a truly terrific starting five. And, if it pitches as constituted through the season—well, no, there aren't many scenarios where this goes sideways for the Indians. Pitchers, however, are pitchers! So while it looks great with Corey Kluber, Trevor Bauer, Carlos Carrasco, Clevinger and Shane Bieber soaking up 132 starts, what if 25 or, heaven forbid, 45 of those starts have to be divvied up among Adam Plutko, a debuting Triston McKenzie and comeback-trail Danny Salazar? Maybe it still works, but it gets a lot dicier.

What part of the team can you simply not go along with PECOTA on?

ROB: As much criticism as they deserve for their winter moves (or lack thereof), the one move I liked is the trade for Jake Bauers. PECOTA is smarter than any of us but PECOTA sees Bauers as a below average hitter—with an 89 DRC+. I think Bauers will be much better than that and has the potential to be very solid replacement for Michael Brantley's 2.8 WARP in 2018 while playing solid first base and outfield. His ability to play multiple positions also gives them flexibility if they do want to upgrade the roster this summer.

Any PECOTA shade you want to throw?

ZACH: Can I go with the overall record? Because I'm going to go with the overall record. Look, PECOTA's 97-win calculation is totally within reason—obviously, it has nothing but reason. Still, the Indians could see wins fall away because of some of the things PECOTA doesn't have enough information to fully account for.

Cleveland's bullpen is without Andrew Miller, without Cody Allen. It's not the same one that Terry Francona guided through the recent glory years. Brad Hand appears very solid, but the next best arms are Tyler Olson (whose 27 1/3 innings in 2018 were a career high) and Adam Cimber (whose breakout season wound up with a 4.58 DRA next to it). Now, PECOTA takes their performance with a proper grain of salt, but it might not fully understand the issues bullpen breakdowns could cause for a team that might respond to a blown save by parading Tyler Naquin, Roberto Perez and Greg Allen to the plate for decimation by the opposing closer.

Those potential blind spots also extend, meaningfully, to other AL Central teams. The White Sox are nothing but youngsters waiting to break out or be sent away. The Twins have an injury returnee in Michael Pineda and a breakout starter in Kyle Gibson that are approached cautiously, but who could make that team more formidable.

So, I'll say it: The 97-win projection, uh, projects more confidence than I'd have about this team.

ROB: The bullpen is a great point. It feels like they were on the forefront of the super bullpen movement that has become the en vogue way to build a team. Their bullpen this year sure feels like Brad Hand and 7 guys who have never been in my kitchen. Which is fine if their starters go into the 8th inning every single night, but boy it could go badly. It's interesting because it is the opposite approach to most teams this year—either by design or accident.

The other player I like more than PECOTA is Leonys Martin. Do you realize he was a 3.3 WARP player last year? A dead average 100 DRC+ and very good outfield defense in 353 plate appearances before a rather terrifying life-threatening bacterial infection ended his season. This year PECOTA has him down for 1.6 WARP. Maybe it's the fantasy guy in me talking (Martin was my outfielder to target in fantasy because of his cheap speed/power combo) but I think he'll be closer to last year than what PECOTA sees.

How will this team be improved by the end of the year, through trade or call-ups, compared to their roster now?

ZACH: Martin is definitely a player who got a little lost in the offseason shuffle for the worst possible reason—hopefully he's healthy and a full go. If he can return to his 2018 form, that would be a boon for the outfield we have spent some time maligning here.

I'll mention another player who might help fill in some of the gaps. Oscar Mercado was acquired from the Cardinals at the deadline last year in a weird, all-minor leaguer deal. Converted to the outfield over the past couple years from shortstop, Mercado is knocking on the door and won't have to do a whole heck of a lot to win a look. He makes enough contact and reaches base enough to run like crazy (he stole 38 bases in Double-A in 2017 and 37 in Triple-A last season). If this sounds like Allen, an outfielder whose bat hasn't played at all in the majors thus far, at least know he's got more pop—13 homers in 2017, 8 last year.

Does this system have anyone else intriguing to you, or will we be talking about more under-the-radar Martin-style trades in Cleveland come July?

ROB: Weird as it is to say, a healthy Salazar could become a nice weapon out of the bullpen in the second half. PECOTA sees him as a 3.30 ERA reliever with well over a strikeout an inning. Cleveland would be thrilled to get anything close to that from him. Combine him with top prospect McKenzie down the stretch and maybe it's not too crazy to think they could replicate their super bullpen of days gone by with internal options in time for the playoffs. I'm not sure I'd bet money on that happening, but it's possible.

Low-end trade acquisitions seem far more likely.

What will people remember about your team's 2019 season five years from now?

ROB: Big question: is this the beginning of the end for this Cleveland team? If they tried to trade Kluber and Bauer this winter, it seems even more likely one or both of them will be gone by this time next year? Or is it absurd to talk about windows closing for a team projected to finish 16 games ahead of Minnesota?

ZACH: It seems absurd, doesn't it? Here are some basic things that should power this core toward October for the foreseeable future: Kluber is signed through 2021 if they pick up his very reasonable options (I know I just assumed the Indians would spend $17-18M per year but here's hoping). Ramirez is signed cheaply through 2023, and Lindor is under control through 2021.

On the other hand, Lindor is making $10M this year, his first being eligible for arbitration, and boy could that number skyrocket. We know Bauer won't be giving an inch on his value, nor should he. And the farm system isn't bursting with near-term help outside of McKenzie. Even if they keep cranking out overachieving pitchers via player development a la Clevinger and Bieber, they're going to have to spend or trade from strength to round out this roster at some point.

The most likely path, to me, would seem to be a restocking—either at the deadline or next winter—by trading a pitcher like Bauer. But there are more dramatic courses of action possible. With whispers already hinting at extension friction, how long do you see Lindor (gulp) remaining in an Indians uniform?

ROB: It's such a tough question. If you're Lindor, do you look at the past two winters and say to yourself maybe I sign a long-term deal with Cleveland buying out two of my arbitration years and a couple more years of free agency to avoid the morass of recent free agency or do you assume that 2022 is a long, long time from now and hope that baseball's economic world will make sense again by then? At the very least I think you have to listen if Cleveland calls and offers a contract. Whether Cleveland will spend the money it takes is an annoying but key point.

But for 2020, assume they do cash in Kluber and Bauer for a boatload of young talent. A rotation of Carrasco, Clevinger, Bieber and McKenzie would, you have to think, be competitive in their division if not the favorite. So as bad as their farm system is today, I'm not sure this is the beginning of the end. I can see the path to them rebuilding on the fly—which is what I think they were thinking by shopping Kluber and Bauer. 'We can win the division, get a lottery ticket into the playoffs and ensure we stay competitive well into the next decade.' Crazy or not crazy?

ZACH: Not crazy. I would do everything possible to hold on to Kluber (well, everything except give up on extending Lindor), but the on-the-fly rebuild seems imminently possible. So for now: Window thoroughly open. But that isn't specific enough for us. We need 2019 win totals. For all of the warts on this club, the top-line talent as undeniable as the dearth of competition in the AL Central. Pitching risk and depth questions have me steering south of PECOTA, but still seeing a division crown and 93 wins.

Where do you land?

ROB: As good as Lindor and Ramirez are, a lot of their value has been how healthy they've been, accumulating massive numbers of plate appearances. Lindor's injury worries me a fair bit. But they get to play KC, Detroit and the White Sox an awful lot—that can cover up all kinds of warts. So as flawed as I think we both agree they are, I still see an 89-win team that wins the division pretty easily.

Performance Graphs

2018 Hit List Ranking

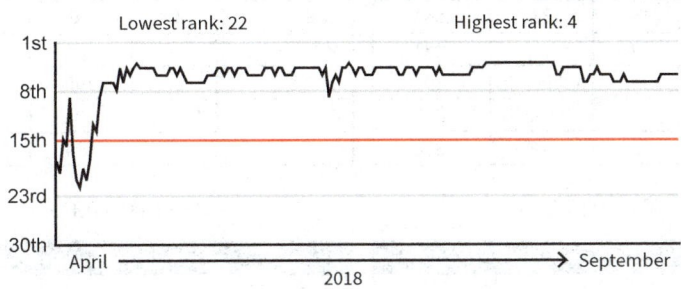

Committed Payroll (in millions)

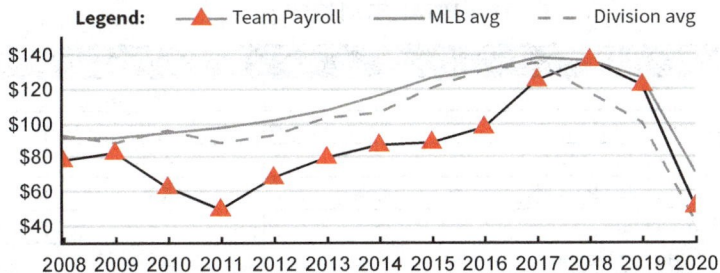

Farm System Ranking

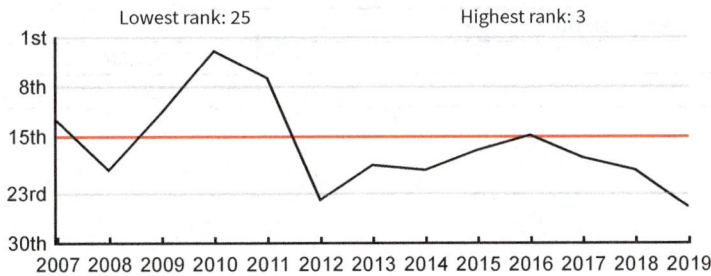

2018 Team Performance

ACTUAL STANDINGS

Team	W	L	Pct
CLE	**91**	**71**	**.561**
MIN	78	84	.481
DET	64	98	.395
CHA	62	100	.382
KCA	58	104	.358

THIRD-ORDER STANDINGS

Team	W	L	Pct
CLE	**92**	**70**	**.567**
MIN	70	92	.432
DET	62	100	.382
CHA	61	101	.376
KCA	58	104	.358

TOP HITTERS

Player	WARP
Jose Ramirez	6.6
Francisco Lindor	6.5
Yan Gomes	3.1

TOP PITCHERS

Player	WARP
Corey Kluber	6.1
Trevor Bauer	5.7
Carlos Carrasco	5.3

VITAL STATISTICS

Statistic Name	Value	Rank
Pythagenpat	.608	5th
Runs Scored per Game	5.05	3rd
Runs Allowed per Game	4.00	7th
Deserved Runs Created Plus	105	6th
Deserved Run Average	3.65	3rd
Fielding Independent Pitching	3.82	5th
Defensive Efficiency Rating	.702	20th
Batter Age	29.3	27th
Pitcher Age	29.2	23rd
Salary	$134.9M	15th
Marginal $ per Marginal Win	$2.9M	23rd
Disabled List Days	$1,207.0M	14th
$ on DL	15%	13th

2019 Team Projections

PROJECTED STANDINGS

Team	W	L	Pct	+/-
CLE	**97**	**65**	**.598**	**+6**
MIN	82	80	.506	+4
KCA	72	90	.444	+14
CHA	70	92	.432	+8
DET	67	95	.413	+3

TOP PROJECTED HITTERS

Player	WARP
Francisco Lindor	5.2
Jose Ramirez	4.9
Roberto Perez	2.6

TOP PROJECTED PITCHERS

Player	WARP
Carlos Carrasco	4.0
Corey Kluber	3.8
Trevor Bauer	3.4

FARM SYSTEM REPORT

Top Prospect	Number of Top 101 Prospects
Triston McKenzie, #43	2

KEY DEDUCTIONS

Player	WARP
Edwin Encarnacion	2.9
Josh Donaldson	2.7
Michael Brantley	1.4
Yandy Diaz	1.4
Lonnie Chisenhall	1.2
Yan Gomes	1.0
Andrew Miller	0.9
Yonder Alonso	0.8
Brandon Guyer	0.4
Cody Allen	0.4
Melky Cabrera	0.3

KEY ADDITIONS

Player	WARP
Carlos Santana	2.1
Matt Joyce	1.5
Jordan Luplow	1.0
Kevin Plawecki	0.7
Hanley Ramirez	0.4
Jake Bauers	0.3

Team Personnel

President
Chris Antonetti

General Manager
Mike Chernoff

Assistant General Manager
Carter Hawkins

Assistant General Manager
Matt Forman

Manager
Terry Francona

BP Alumni
Max Marchi
Ethan Purser
Steffan Segui
Keith Woolner

Progressive Field Stats

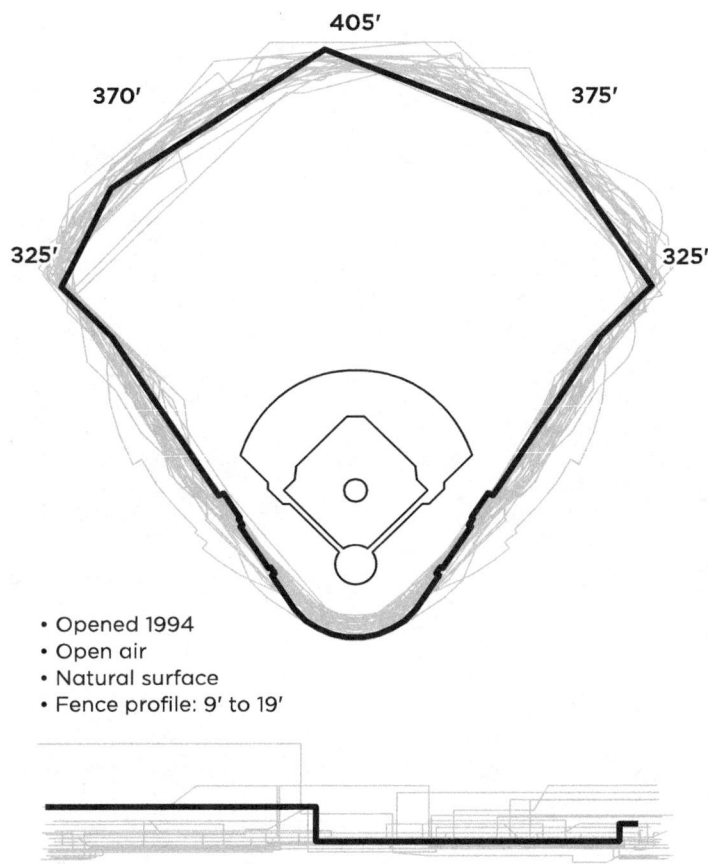

- Opened 1994
- Open air
- Natural surface
- Fence profile: 9' to 19'

Three-Year Park Factors

Runs	Runs/RH	Runs/LH	HR/RH	HR/LH
102	97	113	97	109

Indians Team Analysis

In baseball's pile of unwieldy and unanswerable questions, there's one that pokes out as most unwieldy and unanswerable of all: The question of baseball's purpose. It's far too messy and existential to unpack with any real satisfaction, and unlike many previously unanswerable questions, there's no help to be found in modern analysis and technology. But there are a few related inquiries that will get you pointing in the same general direction, without quite so much metaphysical pressure—the purpose of constructing a professional baseball roster, for instance. It might not seem like there's anything close to a universal answer for this one, but there are a couple starting points. *Winning* seems like an easy pick, but that's not quite specific enough; some teams are built to win this year and some teams are built to win in five years and some teams, really, aren't built to win at all. If that's out, then cost *efficiency* might sound like a more modern choice, but again, that's more of a common answer than a comprehensive one. (For now, at least.) No, the best option for a universal answer is somewhat related to both of these responses, but it's a little different: It's the defense against uncertainty.

No baseball team can ever fully protect itself against uncertainty; there will always be breakouts and breakdowns and blown-out elbows that can't be forecast. PECOTA's always going to miss *something*, and October is all uncertainty for all involved. But a team can still build a defense here, no matter what its precise greater goal might be. If the desired outcome is winning a championship, they can invest in the best players available. If it's winning a championship while spending the smallest sum necessary, they can try investing in everything other than the conventionally "best" players. If there's not enough around to set an immediate goal, you can zoom out a few years down the line and focus on the farm system—each individual prospect serves as his own hedge against uncertainty, after all, with his status decided by how strong of a hedge he can be. If the farm's beyond hope, they can sink their efforts into infrastructure, beefing up the operations department or, if all else fails, leasing that brand-new TV screen above center field. None of these is a guarantee; there is nothing that can be a guarantee. But they are all defenses, in one way or another. The uncertainty will always be there, and a team's goal is simply to guard against it.

There's a bit of a caveat here, though. There's no such thing as complete certainty—yet there's still relative certainty, imperfect certainty, a series of outcomes that are logically and realistically too likely not to bet on. This is all that a baseball team can hope for. But that kind of certainty is the product of a million factors, many outside the organization's control. A 100-win team could be perfectly constructed to achieve its goal, and it might still share the division with a 108-win team. Plans can be similarly ruined for a team at the other end of the standings; it's much more difficult to grab a high draft pick if there are multiple other clubs who have made their peace with losing. The best opportunity for certainty in baseball doesn't lie in a team's roster. It lies in a team's division.

By this logic, then, no team can be so certain as the Cleveland Indians. They've won three consecutive division titles; a fourth appears almost unavoidable. The AL Central isn't quite barren, but it's close: In 2018, Cleveland was the only team to win more than 78 games. A few green shoots are beginning to break through, and it wouldn't take an especially large investment to push these along even faster, but by and large, the division remains one great dry patch of cracked earth. It's easy to see how different the landscape might look in a few seasons—perhaps just one or two, even. But for now? Cleveland's set off in its own lush little space, and no other team is particularly close.

There's no greater luxury for a baseball team. It's certainty, but it's also *freedom*. Cleveland's front office entered this winter with the knowledge that they could do nothing, and they'd likely still walk to a division title. Flipped around, it's the knowledge that they could do just about *anything*, and they'd likely still win a division title. The ordinary winter checklist is there, sure—necessary replacements, preferred upgrades, whatever else can be tackled if money and energy and opportunity align. The list does not ever go away. But it does lose its weight. The list is now just a framework to build on; it's no longer a burden to bear. They can check off every single item and then go on to add a few more, just to have the joy of crossing them off. They can let all their free agents walk before crumpling the list into a tight little ball and shoving it in the back of a desk drawer. It doesn't matter. The initial outcome is, in all likelihood, going to be the same: They're going to win the division. But, of course, it does matter—very much. How is this freedom meant to be used, then?

They could treat it as freedom to go all the way in. *If we're all but guaranteed to win the division,* they could think, *we might as well be all but guaranteed to win the World Series.* It's permission to abandon caution and conservatism and just *go*. Again, there's no such thing as a guarantee here. But there's such a thing as a good chance, and if you have a chance as good as this one, why not take it? The conventional modern wisdom is that opportunities for contention arrive in carefully structured windows—opened with deliberate strategy, closed on a timed schedule. This, though, feels less like a window than a door. There is space to walk through, fully upright, without sacrifice or contortion or gimmickry. This is a cheesy inspirational poster brought to life: *What would you try if you knew you could not fail?* You are almost certainly going to be playing in October. Build a team that is as prepared as possible to *win* in October. Perhaps that's an exceptionally deep bullpen, or a modular defense, or an embrace of specialized roster roles like the designated runner. Perhaps it's all of these. There's plenty of space to experiment, because in the interim, there's plenty of space to do *anything*.

That's one line of thinking. Here is another: They could treat it as freedom to strip all the way down. *If we're all but guaranteed to win the division*, they could think, *we might as well sit back and let it happen*. This is very similar to the freedom to do nothing, and it is that, to a certain extent, but it's also the freedom to cut back. It's the freedom to get worse. They're going to win, after all, and that does not hinge on whether they project as a 95-win team or 90-win team or 85-win team. Why not let themselves get a little worse, then—or, in more practical terms, let themselves cut a few costs? They can let the free agents go. They can trade from an area of depth, without being particularly demanding about the return. (It's worth noting that this option does not necessarily mean saving money for its own sake. There's another path here—trading for top-tier prospects, which would likely mean taking on some money, too. It's a path that might feel like taking advantage of an isolated system to build a perpetual motion machine, rather than working to move as little as possible. But this path, it seems, isn't being taken here.) This is the opposite of the cheesy inspirational poster: *What would you do if you knew you didn't have to try?* There's no way to guarantee a win in October. Why try, then? The field will always have better odds than any single team, so what's the point? A division title gets preserved in the rafters, too.

These are different strategies, but they're also different philosophies. They point back to the original question posed here—the purpose of baseball, or, at least, the purpose of constructing a professional baseball roster. They get at the difference between *trying* and *winning*, and whether there is any virtue to be found in the space in between. If the true measure of a person's character is who he or she is when no one is watching, then, perhaps, the true measure of a front office's spirit is what its roster looks like when the division is bad. Of course, this can't be purely a philosophical question; any strategy here must first be filtered through practical constraints. There's the state of free agency, the landscape of trade opportunity, the threat of financial pressure from ownership—any or all of these might play a crucial role. But you can attempt to account for all of that behind the scenes, and you might still find it difficult to look at the result and see anything other than an endorsement of a particular ideology. It is, fundamentally, a measure of how much a team would like to bet on hope rather than against it.

Cleveland began the offseason by trading catcher Yan Gomes to Washington. His $7 million salary for 2019 was handed off for a minor-league outfielder and middling rookie reliever. Gomes' recent performance had been up-and-down, broken up by injuries and fallow stretches. The track record and outlook for his backup, Roberto Perez, was neither decidedly better nor decidedly worse. The obvious in-house replacement and number one prospect, Francisco Mejia, was shipped off at the deadline in 2018, leaving Eric Haase, the top young catcher in his stead, just about ready for the big leagues. The team hasn't shown any strong interest in looking elsewhere for a catcher. Perez and Haase—a decently capable duo, if not a particularly inspiring one—would be enough. The Gomes trade didn't make them better, then, but it didn't make them worse, either. Mostly, it just made them less expensive.

This set the tone for the winter. A three-team trade sent away slugger Edwin Encarnacion and third baseman Yandy Diaz for first baseman Carlos Santana and Jake Bauers. When Encarnacion was signed in 2016, he'd represented the biggest contract in Cleveland's history. Now, the relationship had been unceremoniously discontinued, in exchange for the slightly heftier contract of Santana. There was one key difference, though: Encarnacion's guaranteed money was stuck in 2019 (with a buyout for 2020), while Santana's went through 2019 and 2020 (with a smaller buyout for 2021). Cleveland couldn't dump a large contract outright, but they could spread out their costs over an extra year. Both Encarnacion and Santana have seen better days, though each kept the potential to function as a solid first baseman or DH; Diaz and Bauers similarly represent something close to a wash. Here, again, was a move that made the team not much better nor much worse. It just made them a little less expensive for the immediate future.

Cleveland freed up additional cash by trading first baseman Yonder Alonso to the Chicago White Sox, who agreed to pay in full his salary of $8 million for 2019. They watched one free agent walk after another: Michael Brantley, Andrew Miller, Lonnie Chisenhall. Their payroll cuts did not come with additions or extensions, with one exception. Pitcher Carlos Carrasco was kept on through 2022 on a remarkably team-friendly extension. The 31-year-old was evidently staying put for the long haul—which only served to fuel rumors about what might happen to the team's other starting pitchers, including Corey Kluber and Trevor Bauer. Both were reportedly put up on the trading block. Cleveland's greatest source of depth had been its rotation, and it was now at risk of being dismantled. It's a reasonable move for a team trying to survive, but that doesn't make it an exciting move for a team trying to win.

Cleveland's front office was apparently instructed to cut payroll, and they succeeded. A more optimistic view is that they've achieved financial flexibility; there's a crucial caveat, however, in that financial flexibility is only valuable insofar as it is used to stretch for anything. Given the nature of their trades—major-league salaries exchanged for minor-league talent—it seems that the team is more interested in investing in the future than for the present, without making a dramatic investment in either direction. The winter isn't just a question of philosophy. It's a practical exercise in money, in public relations, in balancing short-term and long-term need. Yet it can be all of that and still, at the same time, register as the picture of a team that didn't have to try and took that as a reason not to.

—*Emma Baccellieri is a staff writer at Sports Illustrated.*

Part 2: Player Analysis

Greg Allen CF

Born: 03/15/93 Age: 26 Bats: B Throws: R
Height: 6'0" Weight: 175 Origin: Round 6, 2014 Draft (#188 overall)

YEAR	TEAM	LVL	AGE	PA	R	2B	3B	HR	RBI	BB	K	SB	CS	AVG/OBP/SLG
2016	LYN	A+	23	432	93	16	4	4	31	58	51	38	7	.298/.424/.402
2016	AKR	AA	23	174	26	7	3	3	13	19	27	7	6	.290/.399/.441
2017	AKR	AA	24	303	37	16	1	2	24	22	55	21	2	.264/.344/.357
2017	CLE	MLB	24	39	7	1	0	1	6	2	8	1	0	.229/.282/.343
2018	COH	AAA	25	205	31	13	0	2	14	19	44	12	6	.298/.395/.409
2018	CLE	MLB	25	291	36	11	3	2	20	14	58	21	4	.257/.310/.343
2019	CLE	MLB	26	360	45	16	2	7	33	25	79	19	5	.252/.318/.380

Breakout: 7% Improve: 44% Collapse: 7% Attrition: 24% MLB: 72%
Comparables: Brett Gardner, Trevor Crowe, Bryan Petersen

Apply a rash of injuries to a Cleveland outfield group which was not very deep to begin with and you have a whole lot of opportunity. Enter Allen, a 25-year-old, speed-first center fielder who already had about 500 Double-A plate appearances heading into the year. Allen showed he can handle center in the bigs and that he can get at his speed in games, stealing 21 bases on 25 attempts and posting a BRR that was just outside the top 25 in baseball in only half a season. Those skills are going to keep buying him chances, but his bat will almost certainly limit him to a bench role barring unforeseen improvement.

YEAR	TEAM	LVL	AGE	PA	DRC+	VORP	BABIP	BRR	FRAA	WARP
2016	LYN	A+	23	432	147	49.4	.338	13.1	CF(92): 15.9	5.2
2016	AKR	AA	23	174	131	16.1	.336	2.3	CF(36): 4.1	1.5
2017	AKR	AA	24	303	93	12.9	.319	1.5	CF(67): -6.4, RF(1): -0.1	-0.4
2017	CLE	MLB	24	39	75	0.5	.259	0.7	CF(21): -0.9, LF(5): -0.1	0.0
2018	COH	AAA	25	205	126	13.1	.389	0.3	CF(42): 2.3, LF(5): -0.4	1.2
2018	CLE	MLB	25	291	79	4.1	.320	3.4	CF(78): 2.8, RF(16): -0.4	0.8
2019	CLE	MLB	26	360	86	8.6	.307	2.1	CF 0, LF 0	0.7

Greg Allen, continued

Batted Ball Distribution

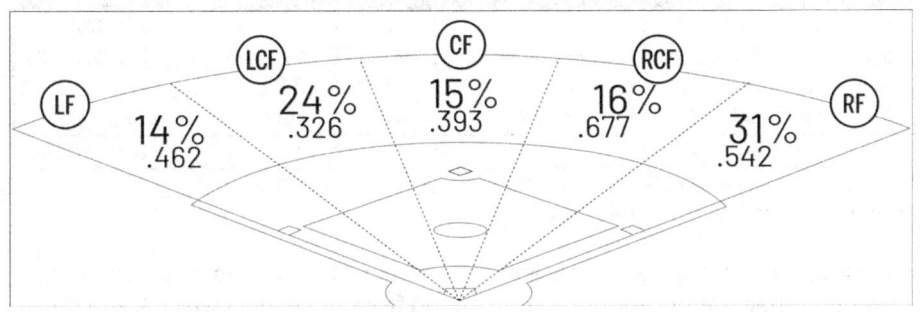

Strike Zone vs LHP   **Strike Zone vs RHP**

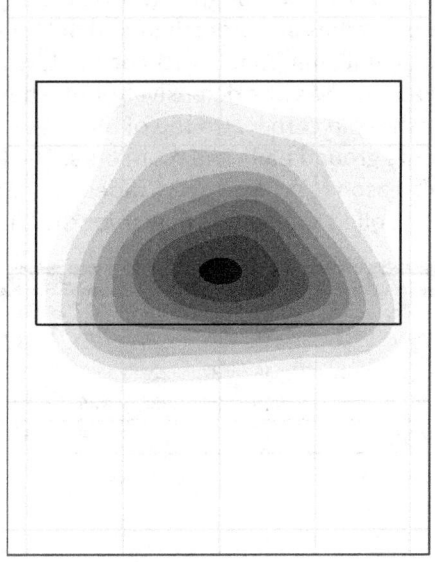

Jake Bauers LF
Born: 10/06/95   Age: 23   Bats: L   Throws: L
Height: 6'1"   Weight: 195   Origin: Round 7, 2013 Draft (#208 overall)

YEAR	TEAM	LVL	AGE	PA	R	2B	3B	HR	RBI	BB	K	SB	CS	AVG/OBP/SLG
2016	MNT	AA	20	581	79	28	1	14	78	73	89	10	6	.274/.370/.420
2017	DUR	AAA	21	575	79	31	1	13	63	78	112	20	3	.263/.368/.412
2018	DUR	AAA	22	222	31	14	0	5	24	23	47	10	6	.279/.357/.426
2018	TBA	MLB	22	388	48	22	2	11	48	54	104	6	6	.201/.316/.384
2019	CLE	MLB	23	546	66	26	2	16	59	59	129	11	5	.226/.316/.390

Breakout: 11%   Improve: 43%   Collapse: 3%   Attrition: 28%   MLB: 60%
Comparables: Casey Kotchman, Daric Barton, Ji-Man Choi

Almost the son of Jack, Bauers made his debut in 2018 after being a figment of Rays fans' imagination since he was acquired from the Padres way back in the Wil Myers trade. Bauers is one of those guys who does a few things well but nothing great. He's an athletic defender at first base and can play the outfield corners competently. He's always shown the ability to hit at a solid clip with some power, although that profile is atypical for first base. Bauers was all of those things in the first half and did little in the second half. His strikeouts rose to an uncommon rate of 30 percent, which basically sunk all of his value at the plate. He was fine defensively, but when's the last time a team went defense first at the cold corner? On top of the strikeouts, he got a bit pull happy, resulting in more ground balls and more outs. The league adjusted to Bauers. He had the offseason to adjust back. Traded to the Indians, he'll look to be a cheap, team-controlled supporting player for the Lindor-Ramirez headliners.

YEAR	TEAM	LVL	AGE	PA	DRC+	VORP	BABIP	BRR	FRAA	WARP
2016	MNT	AA	20	581	137	33.6	.305	2.1	RF(62): 7.2, 1B(57): 0.0	3.0
2017	DUR	AAA	21	575	121	23.7	.314	0.5	LF(55): 4.7, 1B(52): -1.0	2.0
2018	DUR	AAA	22	222	125	12.0	.345	0.9	1B(46): -0.4, LF(4): 0.3	0.6
2018	TBA	MLB	22	388	86	8.5	.252	2.5	1B(76): -2.4, LF(16): 0.5	0.0
2019	CLE	MLB	23	546	88	5.3	.271	-0.3	1B -1, LF 1	0.3

Jake Bauers, continued

Batted Ball Distribution

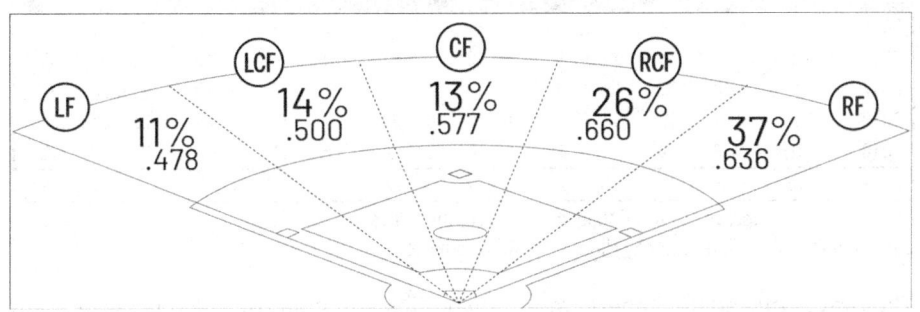

Strike Zone vs LHP   **Strike Zone vs RHP**

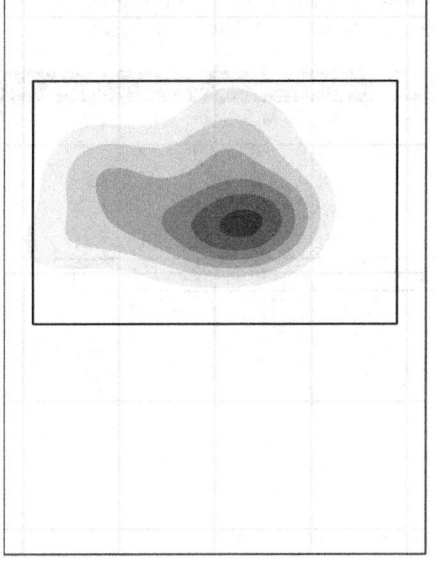

Ryan Flaherty 3B

Born: 07/27/86 Age: 32 Bats: L Throws: R
Height: 6'3" Weight: 220 Origin: Round 1, 2008 Draft (#41 overall)

YEAR	TEAM	LVL	AGE	PA	R	2B	3B	HR	RBI	BB	K	SB	CS	AVG/OBP/SLG
2016	BAL	MLB	29	176	16	7	0	3	15	17	48	2	0	.217/.291/.318
2017	BOW	AA	30	49	18	3	0	2	6	10	3	0	0	.395/.531/.632
2017	BAL	MLB	30	43	5	1	0	0	4	4	10	0	0	.211/.302/.237
2018	GWN	AAA	31	32	3	1	0	0	4	1	9	0	0	.267/.313/.300
2018	ATL	MLB	31	182	17	6	0	2	13	18	41	4	2	.217/.298/.292
2019	CLE	MLB	32	251	25	9	1	5	23	22	59	3	1	.224/.298/.339

Breakout: 3% Improve: 34% Collapse: 14% Attrition: 15% MLB: 88%
Comparables: Ossie Bluege, Pinky Higgins, Chris Woodward

The Braves picked up Flaherty for utility but instead got futility. Expectations surely weren't that high to begin with considering he hit as the same pace as every other season since 2012. Credit to the former first-rounder, though, for carving out a career and having the ability to play all over the field at a solid level. He'll probably keep filling holes for second-division teams until they no longer call him in the offseason.

YEAR	TEAM	LVL	AGE	PA	DRC+	VORP	BABIP	BRR	FRAA	WARP
2016	BAL	MLB	29	176	65	-0.7	.290	1.0	3B(40): 1.0, SS(13): -0.4	0.0
2017	BOW	AA	30	49	188	7.8	.394	1.3	2B(4): -0.2, 3B(4): 0.1	0.7
2017	BAL	MLB	30	43	77	0.5	.286	0.7	2B(12): 0.0, SS(5): -0.3	0.1
2018	GWN	AAA	31	32	66	0.5	.381	0.2	2B(3): -0.1, SS(2): 0.9	0.0
2018	ATL	MLB	31	182	67	-1.0	.277	1.9	3B(40): -0.4, 1B(7): -0.1	0.0
2019	CLE	MLB	32	251	73	-0.7	.280	1.2	3B -1, 1B 0	-0.2

Ryan Flaherty, continued

Batted Ball Distribution

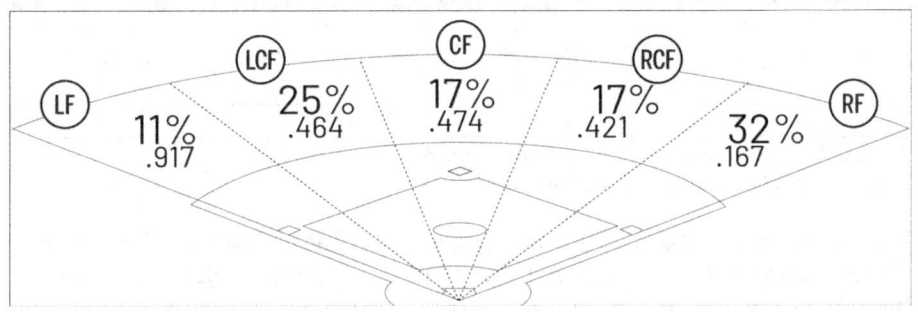

Strike Zone vs LHP   Strike Zone vs RHP

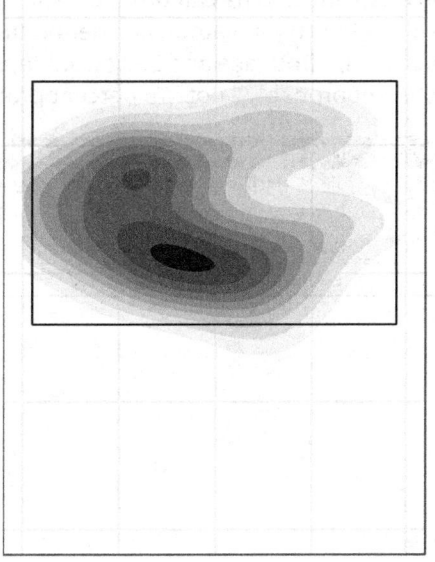

Matt Joyce LF

Born: 08/03/84 Age: 34 Bats: L Throws: R
Height: 6'2" Weight: 205 Origin: Round 12, 2005 Draft (#360 overall)

YEAR	TEAM	LVL	AGE	PA	R	2B	3B	HR	RBI	BB	K	SB	CS	AVG/OBP/SLG
2016	PIT	MLB	31	293	45	10	1	13	42	59	67	1	1	.242/.403/.463
2017	OAK	MLB	32	544	78	33	0	25	68	66	113	4	1	.243/.335/.473
2018	OAK	MLB	33	246	34	9	0	7	15	35	53	0	2	.208/.322/.353
2019	CLE	MLB	34	298	38	14	1	9	33	35	65	1	1	.239/.333/.411

Breakout: 1%   Improve: 23%   Collapse: 24%   Attrition: 15%   MLB: 91%
Comparables: Willie Harris, Jose Cruz Jr., Alex Gordon

Joyce suffered about as bad an entry to free agency as a player can, hitting the disabled list with a back problem twice, ultimately spending over 40 percent of the season inactive. He returned when rosters expanded, but was in the starting lineup just once in September as Nick Martini supplanted him as the A's main lefty left fielder. As miserable as "replaced by Nick Martini" sounds, and as bad as Joyce's final line looks, it's nowhere near the depths of his 2015 horror show in Anaheim, and he can probably still help a big-league team as long as it's willing to carry a platoon partner on the bench. That "probably" includes hedges for both age and back trouble, which means we're looking at "50.2 percent probably," not "75 percent probably."

YEAR	TEAM	LVL	AGE	PA	DRC+	VORP	BABIP	BRR	FRAA	WARP
2016	PIT	MLB	31	293	121	22.6	.285	2.6	RF(43): -1.7, LF(26): -0.3	1.5
2017	OAK	MLB	32	544	108	17.9	.263	1.9	RF(115): 0.6, LF(24): 2.4	2.3
2018	OAK	MLB	33	246	98	4.6	.242	0.1	LF(49): 2.0, RF(6): -0.3	0.7
2019	CLE	MLB	34	298	107	11.9	.282	1.0	LF 2, RF 0	1.5

Matt Joyce, continued

Batted Ball Distribution

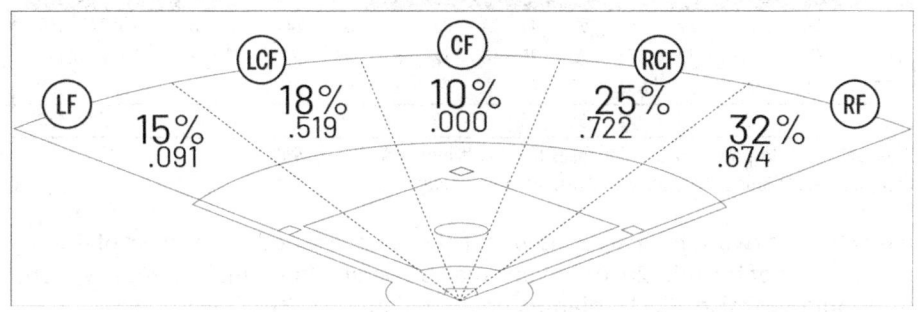

Strike Zone vs LHP   Strike Zone vs RHP

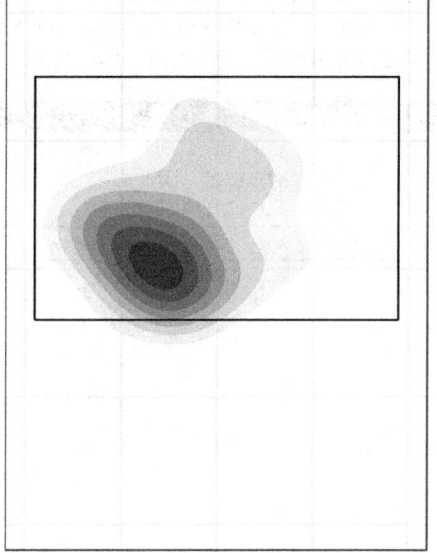

Jason Kipnis 2B

Born: 04/03/87   Age: 32   Bats: L   Throws: R
Height: 5'11"   Weight: 195   Origin: Round 2, 2009 Draft (#63 overall)

YEAR	TEAM	LVL	AGE	PA	R	2B	3B	HR	RBI	BB	K	SB	CS	AVG/OBP/SLG
2016	CLE	MLB	29	688	91	41	4	23	82	60	146	15	3	.275/.343/.469
2017	CLE	MLB	30	373	43	25	0	12	35	28	71	6	2	.232/.291/.414
2018	CLE	MLB	31	601	65	28	1	18	75	60	112	7	1	.230/.315/.389
2019	CLE	MLB	32	471	55	25	2	13	52	40	95	7	2	.249/.319/.410

Breakout: 1%   Improve: 29%   Collapse: 13%   Attrition: 6%   MLB: 94%
Comparables: Orlando Hudson, Mark Ellis, Adam Kennedy

We now have two subpar seasons worth of evidence that the best days of the grindy heart of the mid-2010s Indians may be behind him. Unlike a 2017 season that could optimistically be blamed on myriad injuries, Kipnis was mostly healthy in 2018, but found himself as the weak link in an infield that featured two MVP candidates. So what gives? Kipnis is now well onto the downward slope of an aging curve that's scarcely kind to anyone, let alone second basemen, and his defense there has become suspect enough that Cleveland has tried him in the outfield on occasion. His already deteriorating bat becomes a lot less appealing if moved to a corner outfield spot or first base.

YEAR	TEAM	LVL	AGE	PA	DRC+	VORP	BABIP	BRR	FRAA	WARP
2016	CLE	MLB	29	688	106	24.1	.324	3.0	2B(151): 10.6	4.0
2017	CLE	MLB	30	373	85	6.6	.256	-0.7	2B(75): 1.0, CF(11): -1.1	0.4
2018	CLE	MLB	31	601	94	11.2	.258	-1.2	2B(131): -0.5, CF(14): -2.0	1.1
2019	CLE	MLB	32	471	93	12.8	.289	0.1	2B 3	1.5

Jason Kipnis, continued

Batted Ball Distribution

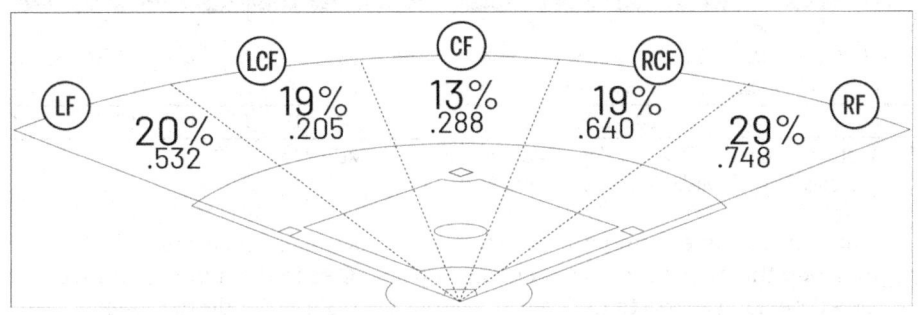

Strike Zone vs LHP   Strike Zone vs RHP

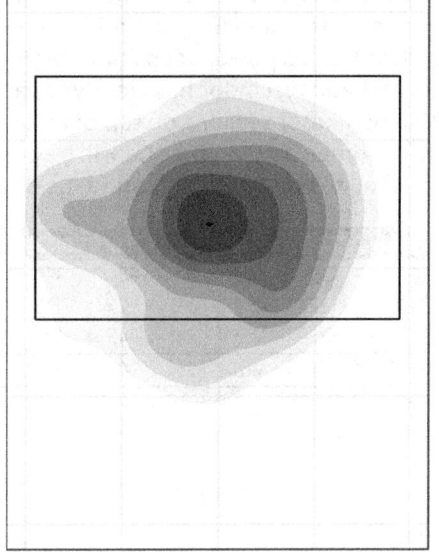

Indians Player Analysis - 31

Francisco Lindor SS

Born: 11/14/93 Age: 25 Bats: B Throws: R
Height: 5'11" Weight: 190 Origin: Round 1, 2011 Draft (#8 overall)

YEAR	TEAM	LVL	AGE	PA	R	2B	3B	HR	RBI	BB	K	SB	CS	AVG/OBP/SLG
2016	CLE	MLB	22	684	99	30	3	15	78	57	88	19	5	.301/.358/.435
2017	CLE	MLB	23	723	99	44	4	33	89	60	93	15	3	.273/.337/.505
2018	CLE	MLB	24	745	129	42	2	38	92	70	107	25	10	.277/.352/.519
2019	CLE	MLB	25	606	92	33	3	24	76	54	85	17	6	.287/.356/.493

Breakout: 4%   Improve: 59%   Collapse: 4%   Attrition: 0%   MLB: 99%
Comparables: Troy Tulowitzki, George Brett, Jose Reyes

Scouting the stat line would not have told you enough about Lindor as he approached the majors. He never cracked an .800 OPS in the minors, and scouts observed he had started to look almost bored in Triple-A. Credit to Cleveland for promoting him instead of letting him languish to teach him some sort of lesson. When he arrived, he was part of a trio of exciting rookies at shortstop along with Carlos Correa and Corey Seager, and there was fun debate about which would be the best. Lindor's ace in the hole seemed to be his elite defense, as set against Correa and Seager's middle-of-the-order thump. The elite defense was real, but as his power keeps blossoming without sacrificing too much of his contact ability, Lindor has clearly separated himself, posting back-to-back 30-plus-homer seasons on top of all the other things he does so magnificently. By the time you read this, he will be barely 25. If you could pick anyone in baseball to build a team around, he'd be in the mix for the no. 1 pick.

YEAR	TEAM	LVL	AGE	PA	DRC+	VORP	BABIP	BRR	FRAA	WARP
2016	CLE	MLB	22	684	110	40.4	.324	5.5	SS(155): 19.3	6.4
2017	CLE	MLB	23	723	118	48.4	.275	2.1	SS(158): 3.8	5.5
2018	CLE	MLB	24	745	128	58.6	.279	-0.5	SS(157): 5.9	6.5
2019	CLE	MLB	25	606	125	44.9	.296	0.9	SS 8	5.2

Francisco Lindor, continued

Batted Ball Distribution

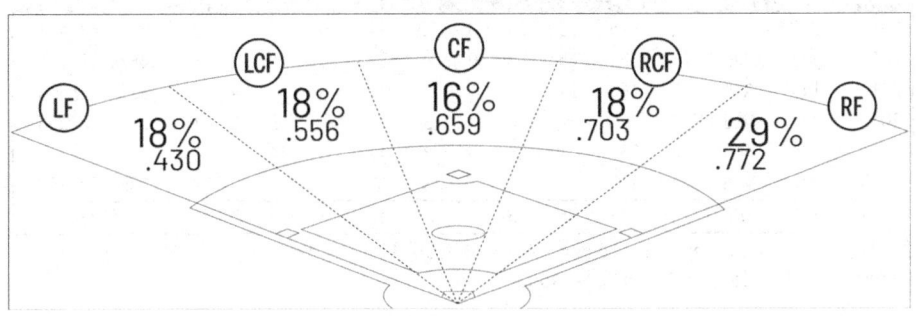

Strike Zone vs LHP **Strike Zone vs RHP**

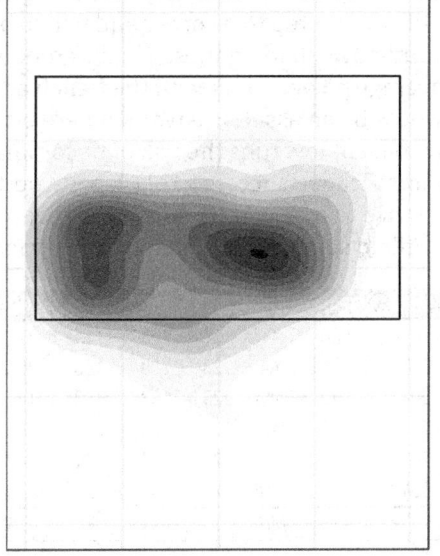

Jordan Luplow LF

Born: 09/26/93 Age: 25 Bats: R Throws: R
Height: 6'1" Weight: 195 Origin: Round 3, 2014 Draft (#100 overall)

YEAR	TEAM	LVL	AGE	PA	R	2B	3B	HR	RBI	BB	K	SB	CS	AVG/OBP/SLG
2016	BRD	A+	22	425	63	23	3	10	54	60	78	6	2	.254/.363/.421
2017	ALT	AA	23	288	45	15	0	16	37	29	45	1	3	.287/.368/.535
2017	IND	AAA	23	182	29	7	1	7	19	16	36	4	1	.325/.401/.513
2017	PIT	MLB	23	87	6	3	1	3	11	6	22	0	1	.205/.276/.385
2018	IND	AAA	24	357	41	25	3	8	49	39	64	7	2	.287/.367/.462
2018	PIT	MLB	24	103	16	1	3	3	7	10	18	2	2	.185/.272/.359
2019	CLE	MLB	25	412	45	18	2	12	47	37	88	4	2	.237/.313/.395

Breakout: 17% Improve: 52% Collapse: 6% Attrition: 33% MLB: 83%
Comparables: Matt LaPorta, Austin Slater, Yonder Alonso

Luplow's 2018 was a mirror image of his 2017. The Fresno State product terrorized pitchers in the minors, then struggled with the Pirates in a limited sample size. Outside of his discipline at the plate, nothing from Triple-A translated to the majors, which isn't good news for a player whose defensive utility is limited to a corner and who'll be more of an asset with the stick against southpaws than righties. In a different era, a right-handed masher with above-average power coming off the bench as a pinch-hitter and occasional starter would be an asset. In a world where pitchers take up 12-13 spot on a 25-man roster, Luplow runs the risk of becoming a Quad-A bat if he doesn't translate minor-league success to big-league performance in short order. Luplow could survive as a bench bat on a team that has the flexibility to move a corner-outfield starter into center when needed. Unfortunately, this is not that team.

YEAR	TEAM	LVL	AGE	PA	DRC+	VORP	BABIP	BRR	FRAA	WARP
2016	BRD	A+	22	425	135	22.1	.294	0.2	LF(81): 7.5	2.2
2017	ALT	AA	23	288	148	25.5	.294	1.5	LF(65): 4.3, 3B(1): 0.0	2.2
2017	IND	AAA	23	182	159	18.2	.381	-0.8	LF(27): 3.4, RF(15): 0.9	1.6
2017	PIT	MLB	23	87	77	-1.2	.241	-0.4	RF(14): 0.1, LF(10): 0.7	0.0
2018	IND	AAA	24	357	141	20.4	.336	-1.7	LF(41): 4.3, RF(38): 1.4	2.3
2018	PIT	MLB	24	103	85	-2.7	.197	-0.4	LF(16): 5.4, RF(11): -0.3	0.6
2019	CLE	MLB	25	412	95	8.1	.280	-0.5	LF 4, RF -2	1.0

Jordan Luplow, continued

Batted Ball Distribution

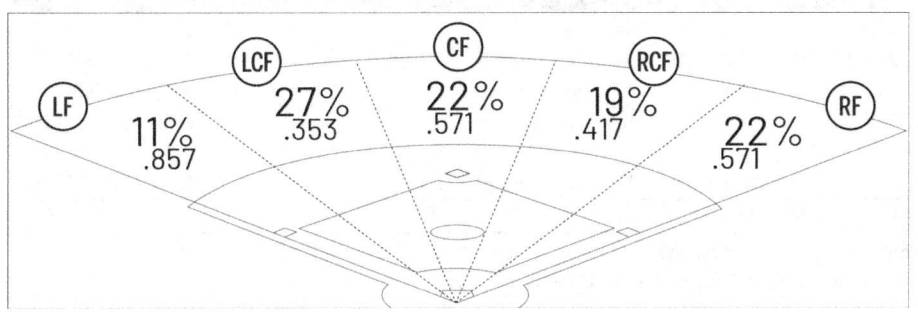

Strike Zone vs LHP   **Strike Zone vs RHP**

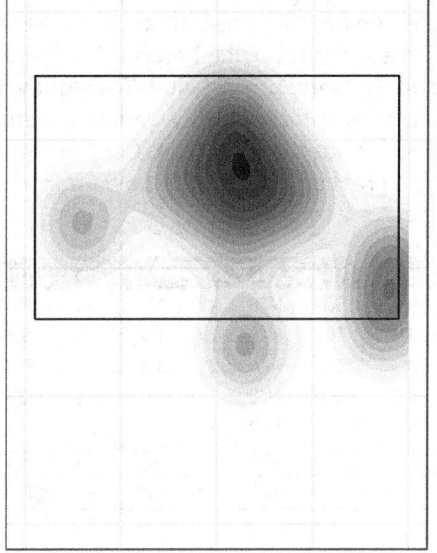

Leonys Martin CF

Born: 03/06/88 Age: 31 Bats: L Throws: R
Height: 6'2" Weight: 200 Origin: International Free Agent, 2011

YEAR	TEAM	LVL	AGE	PA	R	2B	3B	HR	RBI	BB	K	SB	CS	AVG/OBP/SLG
2016	SEA	MLB	28	576	72	17	3	15	47	44	149	24	6	.247/.306/.378
2017	SEA	MLB	29	122	12	2	1	3	8	5	29	6	4	.174/.221/.287
2017	TAC	AAA	29	388	63	24	5	11	39	21	89	25	6	.306/.346/.492
2017	CHN	MLB	29	16	2	1	0	0	1	3	4	1	0	.154/.313/.231
2018	DET	MLB	30	336	45	15	3	9	29	29	75	7	3	.251/.321/.409
2018	CLE	MLB	30	17	3	0	0	2	4	1	2	0	1	.333/.353/.733
2019	CLE	MLB	31	558	76	25	3	16	56	39	135	20	7	.252/.310/.407

Breakout: 0% Improve: 41% Collapse: 15% Attrition: 10% MLB: 86%
Comparables: Nyjer Morgan, Austin Jackson, Rajai Davis

The story of Martin's season was supposed to be one of reclamation. After years of unfulfilled potential bouncing from org to org as a speed/defense guy who couldn't handle the bat well enough to stay in the lineup, Martin signed with the rebuilding Tigers and combined elite defense in center field with a competent enough bat that the contending Indians traded for him. He played only 17 games with the Tribe before a bacterial infection that affected multiple internal organs nearly proved fatal. Thankfully, Martin is expected to make a full recovery and reportedly wanted to return before the season ended, though doctors advised against it. Continuing that progress he showed in 2018 would be a great story, but right now for Martin, baseball understandably takes a back seat.

YEAR	TEAM	LVL	AGE	PA	DRC+	VORP	BABIP	BRR	FRAA	WARP
2016	SEA	MLB	28	576	82	10.7	.313	2.5	CF(143): 9.6	1.9
2017	SEA	MLB	29	122	64	-7.6	.205	-0.4	CF(15): -0.8, RF(15): 2.8	0.0
2017	TAC	AAA	29	388	105	25.8	.376	1.1	CF(82): 16.2	2.8
2017	CHN	MLB	29	16	66	-0.5	.222	0.1	CF(5): 0.0, LF(4): -0.1	-0.1
2018	DET	MLB	30	336	100	11.9	.305	0.7	CF(74): 18.5	3.2
2018	CLE	MLB	30	17	98	2.3	.250	0.4	CF(5): 0.1, RF(1): 0.0	0.1
2019	CLE	MLB	31	558	87	11.5	.308	1.6	CF 5, RF 1	1.6

Leonys Martin, continued

Batted Ball Distribution

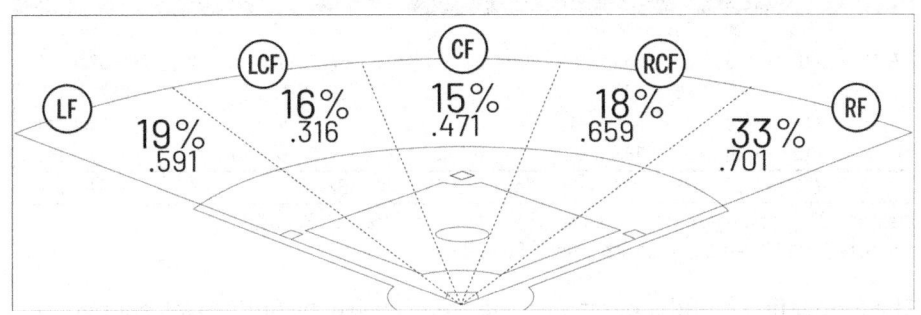

Strike Zone vs LHP   **Strike Zone vs RHP**

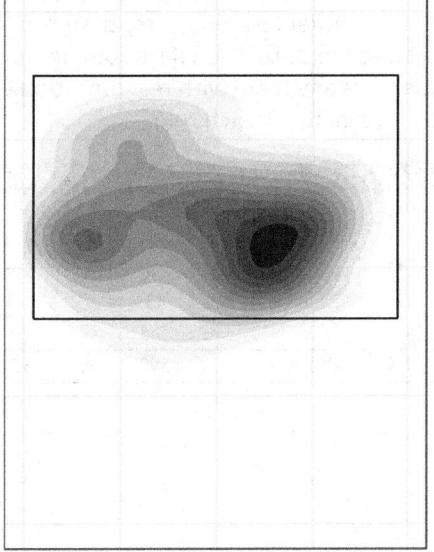

Tyler Naquin RF

Born: 04/24/91 Age: 28 Bats: L Throws: R
Height: 6'2" Weight: 195 Origin: Round 1, 2012 Draft (#15 overall)

YEAR	TEAM	LVL	AGE	PA	R	2B	3B	HR	RBI	BB	K	SB	CS	AVG/OBP/SLG
2016	COH	AAA	25	79	6	3	1	1	8	8	15	1	2	.286/.354/.400
2016	CLE	MLB	25	365	52	18	5	14	43	36	112	6	3	.296/.372/.514
2017	COH	AAA	26	330	42	14	4	10	51	30	71	5	2	.298/.359/.475
2017	CLE	MLB	26	40	4	2	0	0	1	2	9	0	1	.216/.250/.270
2018	CLE	MLB	27	183	22	7	0	3	23	6	42	1	1	.264/.295/.356
2019	CLE	MLB	28	392	45	16	2	12	44	32	102	4	2	.249/.315/.407

Breakout: 3% Improve: 46% Collapse: 15% Attrition: 21% MLB: 88%
Comparables: Will Venable, Nate Schierholtz, Travis Buck

The former first rounder burst onto the scene in 2016 by hitting well enough to overlook his inadequate glove in center field. After his 2017 was lost to woeful ineffectiveness and injury, Naquin's age-27 season began to take on the look of a make-or-break one. While he hit better in his limited looks, his production was still nowhere near his rookie numbers. Perhaps it's fitting that, like Naquin, low-power outfielders who carry their profile with plus corner defense had a moment in 2016. Even if Naquin fights his way back into an everyday job, one suspects any team with real ambition will always be trying to upgrade him or shunt him to a bench role.

YEAR	TEAM	LVL	AGE	PA	DRC+	VORP	BABIP	BRR	FRAA	WARP
2016	COH	AAA	25	79	121	3.1	.345	-1.6	CF(15): 1.3, RF(2): -0.1	0.3
2016	CLE	MLB	25	365	105	18.0	.411	-2.3	CF(105): -8.2, RF(4): -0.4	0.3
2017	COH	AAA	26	330	119	18.7	.358	0.9	CF(49): 10.7, RF(23): -1.1	2.1
2017	CLE	MLB	26	40	73	-1.4	.276	-0.2	CF(11): -0.4, RF(8): -0.5	-0.1
2018	CLE	MLB	27	183	79	1.4	.331	1.0	RF(39): 5.2, CF(19): 0.2	0.6
2019	CLE	MLB	28	392	90	6.2	.313	-0.4	RF 6, LF 0	1.1

Tyler Naquin, continued

Batted Ball Distribution

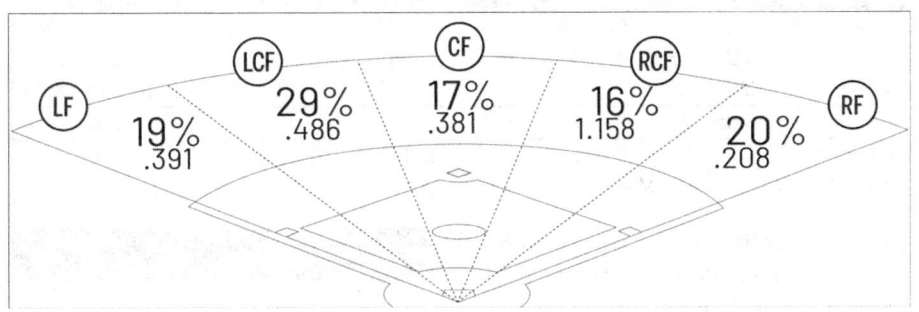

Strike Zone vs LHP **Strike Zone vs RHP**

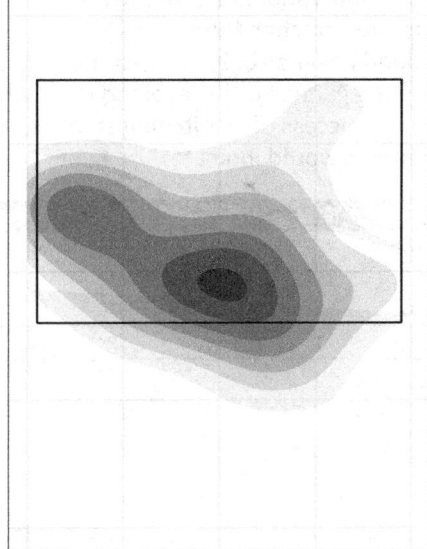

Roberto Perez C

Born: 12/23/88   Age: 30   Bats: R   Throws: R
Height: 5'11"   Weight: 220   Origin: Round 33, 2008 Draft (#1011 overall)

YEAR	TEAM	LVL	AGE	PA	R	2B	3B	HR	RBI	BB	K	SB	CS	AVG/OBP/SLG
2016	CLE	MLB	27	184	14	6	1	3	17	23	44	0	0	.183/.285/.294
2017	CLE	MLB	28	248	22	12	0	8	38	26	71	0	1	.207/.291/.373
2018	CLE	MLB	29	210	16	9	1	2	19	21	70	1	0	.168/.256/.263
2019	CLE	MLB	30	397	38	16	1	9	40	39	107	1	0	.218/.301/.349

Breakout: 7%   Improve: 37%   Collapse: 9%   Attrition: 19%   MLB: 88%
Comparables: Landon Powell, Martin Maldonado, Jose Lobaton

Over the past five seasons, the former 33rd-round pick has never appeared in even half of his team's games nor made 250 trips to the plate, but that may change in 2019 following the trade of Yan Gomes. Why has Perez never had a shot at starting? Well, he hits like a pitcher. But Perez sticks around because of his consistently solid pitch-framing and ability to stymie the running game. For a Cleveland team whose success has mostly been predicated on the success of its pitching staff, he's been more valuable than the raw numbers would indicate.

YEAR	TEAM	P. COUNT	FRM RUNS	BLK RUNS	THRW RUNS	TOT RUNS
2016	CLE	7261	7.7	1.3	1.2	10.8
2016	CLE	7261	7.7	1.3	1.2	10.8
2017	CLE	9658	17.6	2.2	0.4	19.7
2018	CLE	7861	10.9	1.6	-0.2	12.1
2019	CLE	15355	21.3	2.8	0.3	24.5

YEAR	TEAM	LVL	AGE	PA	DRC+	VORP	BABIP	BRR	FRAA	WARP
2016	CLE	MLB	27	184	69	0.2	.229	-0.2	C(61): 10.1	1.2
2017	CLE	MLB	28	248	80	3.6	.266	-0.6	C(71): 19.8	2.5
2018	CLE	MLB	29	210	52	-4.4	.257	-0.2	C(58): 11.1	0.9
2019	CLE	MLB	30	397	73	5.5	.275	-0.6	C 22	2.6

Roberto Perez, continued

Batted Ball Distribution

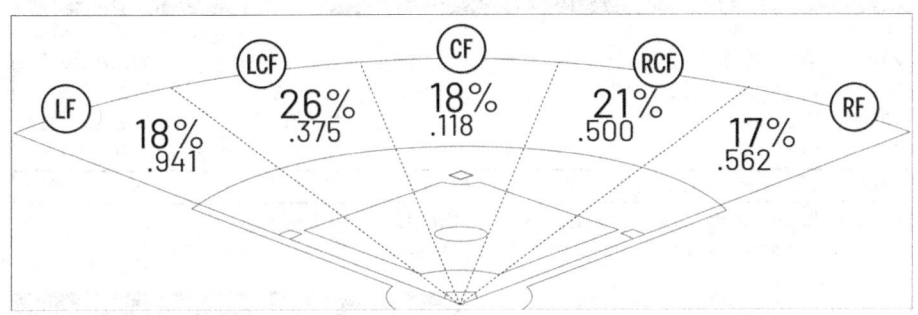

Strike Zone vs LHP   Strike Zone vs RHP

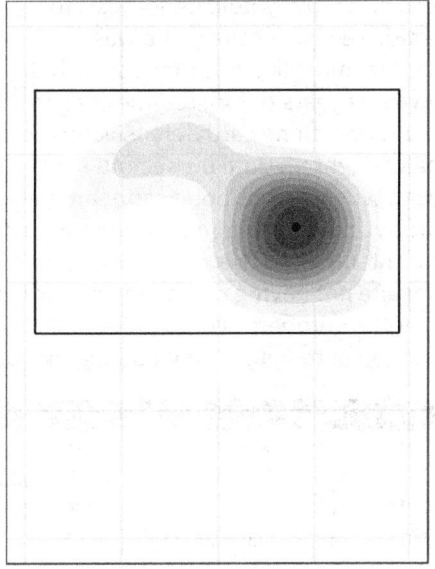

Kevin Plawecki   C

Born: 02/26/91   Age: 28   Bats: R   Throws: R
Height: 6'2"   Weight: 210   Origin: Round 1, 2012 Draft (#35 overall)

YEAR	TEAM	LVL	AGE	PA	R	2B	3B	HR	RBI	BB	K	SB	CS	AVG/OBP/SLG
2016	LVG	AAA	25	207	27	11	0	8	40	13	19	0	1	.300/.348/.484
2016	NYN	MLB	25	151	6	6	0	1	11	17	33	0	0	.197/.298/.265
2017	LVG	AAA	26	275	37	17	1	9	45	16	38	0	0	.328/.375/.514
2017	NYN	MLB	26	118	11	5	0	3	13	14	17	1	0	.260/.364/.400
2018	NYN	MLB	27	277	33	13	2	7	30	28	65	0	1	.210/.315/.370
2019	CLE	MLB	28	196	21	9	1	5	21	16	39	0	0	.246/.321/.394

Breakout: 4%   Improve: 43%   Collapse: 9%   Attrition: 15%   MLB: 84%
Comparables: Ronny Paulino, Martin Maldonado, Jett Bandy

For a slow-footed backstop, Plawecki sure can be elusive. Each time we think we've got him figured out, something in his numbers changes and blows our whole hypothesis to smithereens. In college, he was a contact machine, but those skills hid away for years before re-emerging in 2017. His calling card defensively was getting extra strikes and blocking errant balls—right up until his second consecutive poor season behind the plate this year. When his hit tool disappeared again in 2018, he upped his power production and put more and more batted balls on the ground (yes, simultaneously). He's been trying on a double-digit walk rate for size in Queens despite not having one at any minor-league stop. The only real consistency is that the numbers always point to Plawecki as a prototypical backup catcher. It's just tough to figure out what kind of backup catcher he is.

YEAR	TEAM	P. COUNT	FRM RUNS	BLK RUNS	THRW RUNS	TOT RUNS
2016	NYN	5670	7.1	0.9	-0.2	7.6
2017	LVG	9115	8.7	0.8	-0.4	8.6
2017	NYN	3842	-3.2	0.7	-0.6	-3.3
2018	NYN	9839	-4.6	2.0	0.0	-2.7
2019	CLE	7347	-0.9	0.7	-0.3	-0.5

YEAR	TEAM	LVL	AGE	PA	DRC+	VORP	BABIP	BRR	FRAA	WARP
2016	LVG	AAA	25	207	115	9.9	.297	-1.9	C(41): 4.2, 1B(5): 0.2	1.1
2016	NYN	MLB	25	151	69	2.3	.255	0.3	C(45): 7.4	1.0
2017	LVG	AAA	26	275	126	22.0	.350	-1.4	C(63): 10.7	2.8
2017	NYN	MLB	26	118	101	8.5	.284	-0.3	C(29): -3.3, P(2): 0.0	0.2
2018	NYN	MLB	27	277	92	11.3	.257	-1.2	C(71): -2.0, 1B(3): 0.0	0.8
2019	CLE	MLB	28	196	97	8.4	.289	-0.3	C -1	0.7

Kevin Plawecki, continued

Batted Ball Distribution

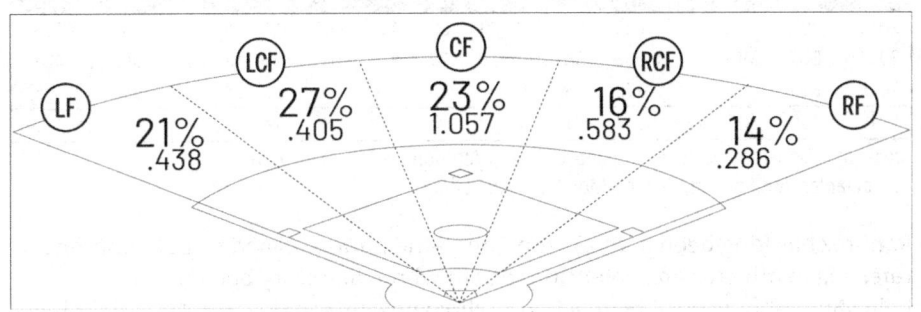

Strike Zone vs LHP   **Strike Zone vs RHP**

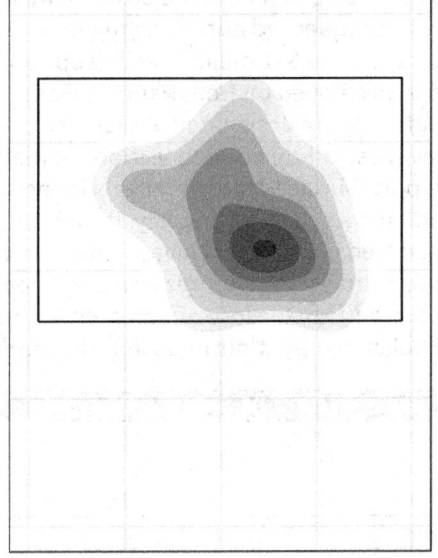

Hanley Ramirez DH

Born: 12/23/83   Age: 35   Bats: R   Throws: R
Height: 6'2"   Weight: 235   Origin: International Free Agent, 2000

YEAR	TEAM	LVL	AGE	PA	R	2B	3B	HR	RBI	BB	K	SB	CS	AVG/OBP/SLG
2016	BOS	MLB	32	620	81	28	1	30	111	60	120	9	3	.286/.361/.505
2017	BOS	MLB	33	553	58	24	0	23	62	51	116	1	3	.242/.320/.429
2018	BOS	MLB	34	195	25	7	0	6	29	14	35	4	1	.254/.313/.395
2019	CLE	MLB	35	257	31	11	1	9	32	26	52	3	1	.251/.336/.418

Breakout: 1%   Improve: 23%   Collapse: 16%   Attrition: 29%   MLB: 92%
Comparables: Aubrey Huff, Kendrys Morales, Andre Ethier

Ramirez has long been in the Tyson Zone—the phrase coined by Bill Simmons referring to athletes and celebrities about whom any story becomes believable—but in 2018 he reached a whole new level of bizarre. After claiming he wanted to rejoin the 30/30 club, Ramirez got off to a hot start in March and April, hitting .330/.400/.474 with three homers and steals apiece. That's when things got weird. He hit just .163/.200/.300 over the next three weeks en route to a surprising DFA from the Sox on May 25. It made some sense; Ramirez was getting squeezed out of playing time at DH and at first base, and was just 302 PA away from a $22 million vesting option for 2019. But the suddenness with which the Sox moved on from Ramirez was surprising; he'd batted third just two days before being designated. It was also odd that no team took a flier on him as a low-cost, all-upside acquisition. To make matters even stranger, in late June, reports surfaced that Ramirez's friend name-dropped him during a drug bust, and the rumors began to fly. It's important to note that Ramirez was never involved in a criminal investigation and that his name was fully cleared. But if this is truly it for Ramirez as a major leaguer, 2018 was perhaps the strangest possible way to close out an exciting, tumultuous and drama-filled career bookended by stints in Boston that ended abruptly.

YEAR	TEAM	LVL	AGE	PA	DRC+	VORP	BABIP	BRR	FRAA	WARP
2016	BOS	MLB	32	620	126	16.3	.315	-2.8	1B(133): -10.4	1.4
2017	BOS	MLB	33	553	105	-0.1	.272	-1.8	1B(18): -1.1	0.8
2018	BOS	MLB	34	195	93	-0.6	.283	-0.9	1B(25): -1.1	-0.1
2019	CLE	MLB	35	257	111	7.1	.291	-0.9	1B -4	0.4

Hanley Ramirez, continued

Batted Ball Distribution

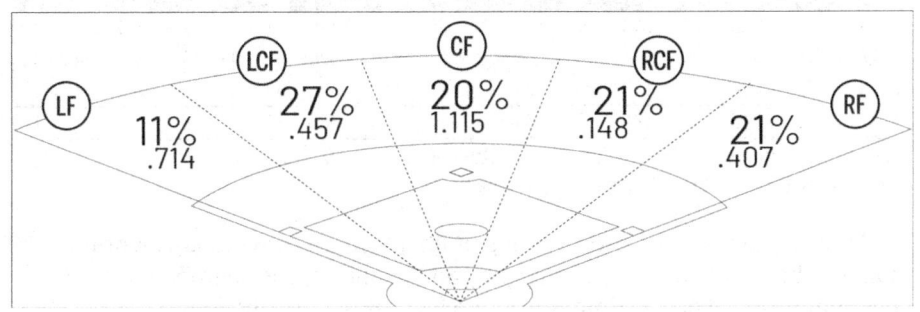

Strike Zone vs LHP   **Strike Zone vs RHP**

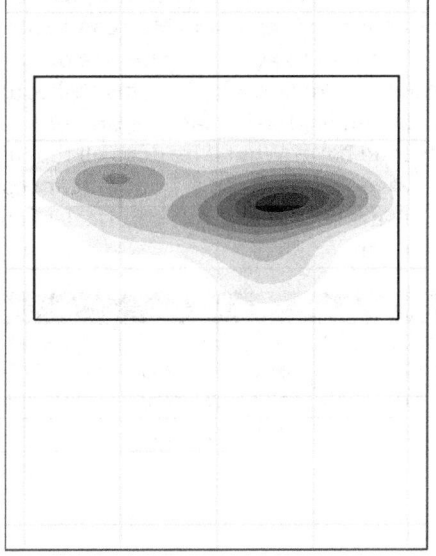

Cleveland Indians 2019

Jose Ramirez INF
Born: 09/17/92 Age: 26 Bats: B Throws: R
Height: 5'9" Weight: 165 Origin: International Free Agent, 2009

YEAR	TEAM	LVL	AGE	PA	R	2B	3B	HR	RBI	BB	K	SB	CS	AVG/OBP/SLG
2016	CLE	MLB	23	618	84	46	3	11	76	44	62	22	7	.312/.363/.462
2017	CLE	MLB	24	645	107	56	6	29	83	52	69	17	5	.318/.374/.583
2018	CLE	MLB	25	698	110	38	4	39	105	106	80	34	6	.270/.387/.552
2019	CLE	MLB	26	648	96	43	4	26	93	68	77	26	6	.303/.381/.531

Breakout: 2% Improve: 61% Collapse: 2% Attrition: 3% MLB: 99%
Comparables: Dustin Pedroia, Wade Boggs, George Brett

You know the old story: Do-everything utility player becomes a fan favorite thanks to his short stature, scrappy play and genuinely rosy demeanor. Those guys come around all the time, stick for a few years — maybe grabbing an everyday job for a year or two — and then spend the rest of their career bouncing around from org to org, the minors and the majors. You're left with your memories and little else. But what if that story turns out differently? What if your scrappy utility player morphs into a middle-of-the-order masher, a bonafide superstar and MVP candidate, terrorizing opposing pitching staffs with elite power to go along with one of the best eyes in the game? What if that power spike doesn't affect his strikeout rate at all? What if he becomes an elite base runner, too? What if he proves he can hold his own at the hot corner or second base? What if he does all that in his age-24 season, does even better in his age-25 season and is under team control for another five years after that? These questions are all rhetorical, of course, because things like that just never happen.

YEAR	TEAM	LVL	AGE	PA	DRC+	VORP	BABIP	BRR	FRAA	WARP
2016	CLE	MLB	23	618	116	31.4	.333	4.7	3B(117): -2.6, LF(48): -0.8	3.3
2017	CLE	MLB	24	645	137	57.1	.319	0.2	3B(88): 6.0, 2B(71): -0.1	5.8
2018	CLE	MLB	25	698	146	70.7	.252	5.2	3B(137): -3.5, 2B(16): -0.7	6.6
2019	CLE	MLB	26	648	142	54.3	.309	2.5	3B -4, 2B -1	4.9

Jose Ramirez, continued

Batted Ball Distribution

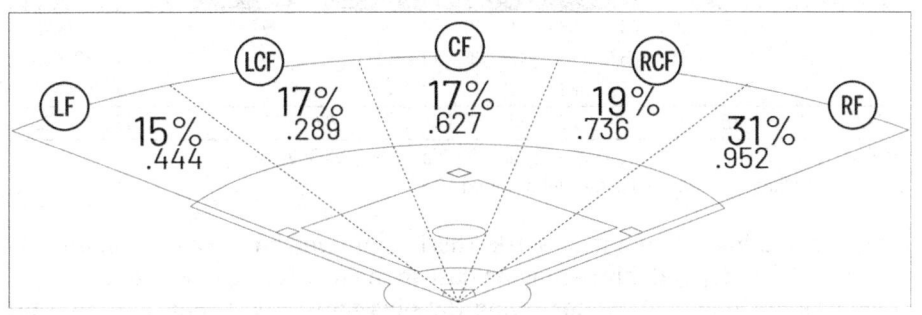

Strike Zone vs LHP   Strike Zone vs RHP

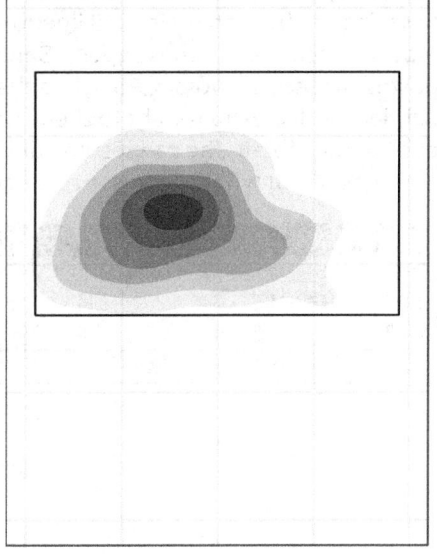

Cleveland Indians 2019

Carlos Santana 1B

Born: 04/08/86 Age: 33 Bats: B Throws: R
Height: 5'11" Weight: 210 Origin: International Free Agent, 2004

YEAR	TEAM	LVL	AGE	PA	R	2B	3B	HR	RBI	BB	K	SB	CS	AVG/OBP/SLG
2016	CLE	MLB	30	688	89	31	3	34	87	99	99	5	2	.259/.366/.498
2017	CLE	MLB	31	667	90	37	3	23	79	88	94	5	1	.259/.363/.455
2018	PHI	MLB	32	679	82	28	2	24	86	110	93	2	1	.229/.352/.414
2019	CLE	MLB	33	600	73	28	2	19	74	80	90	4	1	.248/.353/.422

Breakout: 2% Improve: 22% Collapse: 16% Attrition: 9% MLB: 90%
Comparables: John Jaso, Prince Fielder, John Olerud

It's weird to think of Santana as a risk. This is a guy who hit like a metronome for seven seasons, dependably getting on base in the mid-to-high-.300s and slugging in the mid-.400s while playing 150-plus games and saving a few runs on defense. As far as track records go, Santana's was about as low on the volatility scale as you can get, which certainly made him appealing as a free agent. But the Phillies raced ahead of the pack to sign Santana to a three-year deal, ostensibly and eventually displacing Rhys Hoskins to left field in the name of lowering the beta on their 2018 lineup's expected output. That … didn't exactly play out according to those specs. Santana stayed healthy — 161 games! — but posted his second-worst OPS, while the butterfly effect of installing Hoskins in left field added extra weight to the yoke. Traded briefly to the Mariners and the back to the Indians, he can resume doing his usual thing without anyone worrying about what his presence means for the rest of the roster.

YEAR	TEAM	LVL	AGE	PA	DRC+	VORP	BABIP	BRR	FRAA	WARP
2016	CLE	MLB	30	688	127	20.4	.258	-0.9	1B(64): 4.6	3.6
2017	CLE	MLB	31	667	114	17.5	.274	-1.9	1B(140): 6.2, RF(7): 0.7	2.6
2018	PHI	MLB	32	679	108	25.4	.231	0.2	1B(149): -0.7, 3B(19): 0.6	1.8
2019	CLE	MLB	33	600	112	19.2	.266	-0.7	1B 1	2.1

Carlos Santana, continued

Batted Ball Distribution

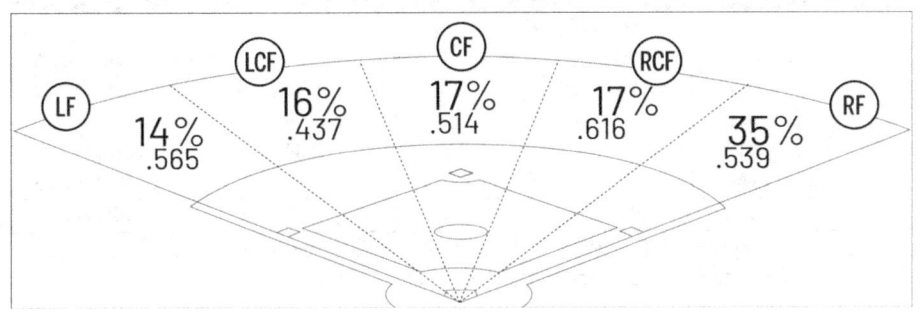

Strike Zone vs LHP   Strike Zone vs RHP

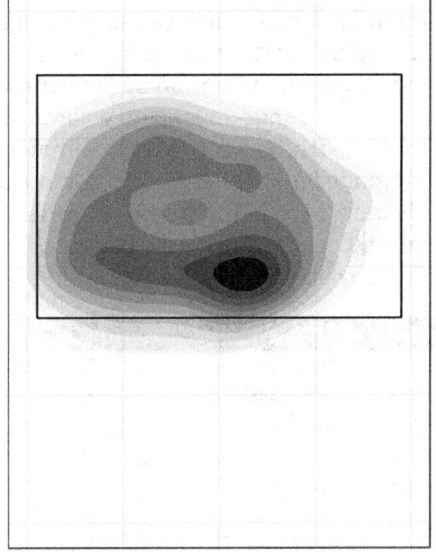

Bradley Zimmer CF
Born: 11/27/92   Age: 26   Bats: L   Throws: R
Height: 6'5"   Weight: 220   Origin: Round 1, 2014 Draft (#21 overall)

YEAR	TEAM	LVL	AGE	PA	R	2B	3B	HR	RBI	BB	K	SB	CS	AVG/OBP/SLG
2016	AKR	AA	23	407	58	20	6	14	53	56	115	33	13	.253/.371/.471
2016	COH	AAA	23	150	18	5	0	1	9	21	56	5	1	.242/.349/.305
2017	COH	AAA	24	144	22	11	2	5	14	14	43	9	3	.294/.371/.532
2017	CLE	MLB	24	332	41	15	2	8	39	26	99	18	1	.241/.307/.385
2018	CLE	MLB	25	114	14	5	0	2	9	7	44	4	1	.226/.281/.330
2018	COH	AAA	25	28	1	0	0	1	1	1	11	1	0	.148/.179/.259
2019	CLE	MLB	26	251	34	9	1	7	22	22	83	12	3	.218/.292/.360

Breakout: 11%   Improve: 48%   Collapse: 11%   Attrition: 24%   MLB: 84%
Comparables: Drew Stubbs, Curtis Granderson, Tyler Naquin

The electric start to Zimmer's major-league career sure does seem like a long time ago. After a 2017 season in which he conquered Triple-A and tore through the majors for the first two months after his promotion, the glaring hole in his hit tool showed up in a major way, first during the second half of the aforementioned rookie campaign and again during the first month of 2018. Handed the starting center fielder job out of spring training, what followed was a rib injury and demotion back to Triple-A, where he lasted only six more games before being shut down with what turned out to be an injured shoulder that required arthroscopic surgery. Zimmer's tool shed is still stocked with the parts that made him a top-101 prospect not all that long ago — speed, power and a solid approach at the plate — but the injury is a significant setback for someone who still needs to prove he can make enough contact to be relied on as an everyday player.

YEAR	TEAM	LVL	AGE	PA	DRC+	VORP	BABIP	BRR	FRAA	WARP
2016	AKR	AA	23	407	127	30.6	.341	1.8	CF(76): -0.3, RF(9): 2.0	2.0
2016	COH	AAA	23	150	87	1.4	.423	-0.7	CF(36): 1.2	0.1
2017	COH	AAA	24	144	127	10.2	.405	-0.6	CF(26): 3.6, RF(8): 0.5	1.0
2017	CLE	MLB	24	332	70	6.8	.328	1.6	CF(97): 9.5	1.0
2018	CLE	MLB	25	114	49	-0.6	.367	1.4	CF(34): 5.4	0.4
2018	COH	AAA	25	28	15	-2.4	.200	0.1	CF(5): -0.2	-0.2
2019	CLE	MLB	26	251	70	1.7	.307	1.5	CF 3	0.5

Bradley Zimmer, continued

Batted Ball Distribution

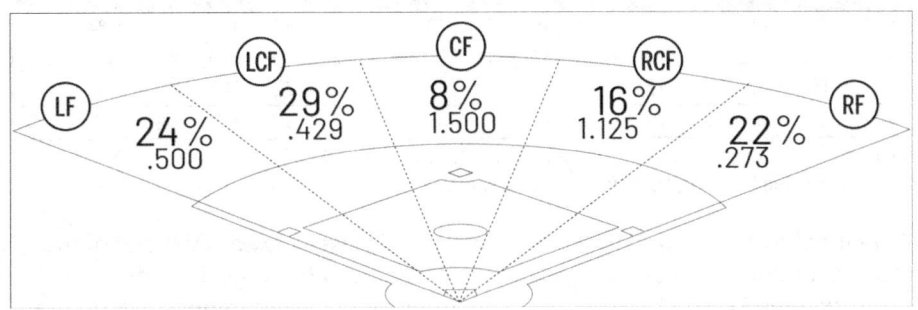

Strike Zone vs LHP   Strike Zone vs RHP

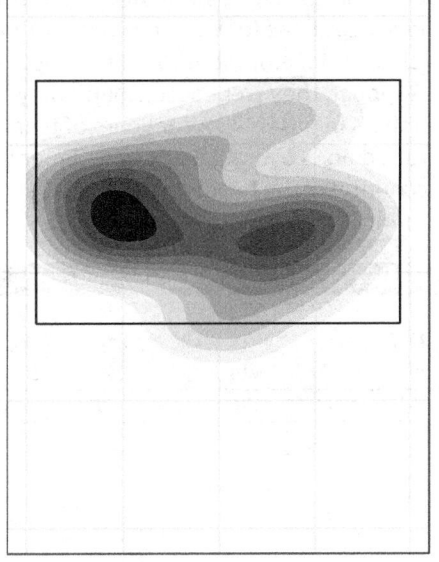

Trevor Bauer   RHP

Born: 01/17/91   Age: 28   Bats: R   Throws: R
Height: 6'1"   Weight: 190   Origin: Round 1, 2011 Draft (#3 overall)

YEAR	TEAM	LVL	AGE	W	L	SV	G	GS	IP	H	HR	BB/9	K/9	K	GB%	BABIP
2016	CLE	MLB	25	12	8	0	35	28	190	179	20	3.3	8.0	168	49%	.292
2017	CLE	MLB	26	17	9	0	32	31	176[1]	181	25	3.1	10.0	196	47%	.337
2018	CLE	MLB	27	12	6	1	28	27	175[1]	134	9	2.9	11.3	221	45%	.297
2019	*CLE*	*MLB*	*28*	*13*	*7*	*0*	*28*	*28*	*168*	*148*	*19*	*3.1*	*10.1*	*189*	*46%*	*.298*

Breakout: 20%   Improve: 57%   Collapse: 25%   Attrition: 6%   MLB: 95%
Comparables: Gio Gonzalez, David Price, Justin Verlander

Were it not for a fractured fibula that cost him six weeks toward the end of the season, it's entirely possible this comment could be about the defending Cy Young winner. Even with the injury, Bauer finished only five innings behind the ultimate winner and was downright dominant when he was on the mound. He proved his strikeout spike from a year earlier was no fluke and even improved upon it while simultaneously suppressing the home run numbers that have long been a nuisance. As someone who throughout the years was more likely to make headlines for what he said on Twitter or where he flew his drone, it was a welcome development for Cleveland. While those headlines didn't exactly disappear, they were accompanied by headlines talking about one of the best pitchers in baseball. After years of teasing with the potential of someone once drafted no. 3 overall, it appears Bauer has paired his consistently delete-your-account-worthy tweets with consistently dominant performances on the mound.

YEAR	TEAM	LVL	AGE	WHIP	ERA	DRA	WARP	MPH	FB%	WHF	CSP
2016	CLE	MLB	25	1.31	4.26	4.60	1.6	96.2	50.9	10.1	47.3
2017	CLE	MLB	26	1.37	4.19	3.95	3.2	96.1	49.3	10.1	44
2018	CLE	MLB	27	1.09	2.21	2.48	5.7	96.4	42.2	14.2	44.3
2019	*CLE*	*MLB*	*28*	*1.23*	*3.29*	*3.78*	*3.2*	*95.7*	*47.1*	*11.8*	*45.2*

Trevor Bauer, continued

Pitch Shape vs LHH

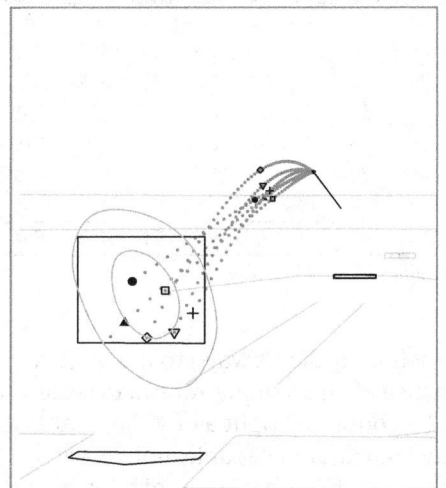

Pitch Shape vs RHH

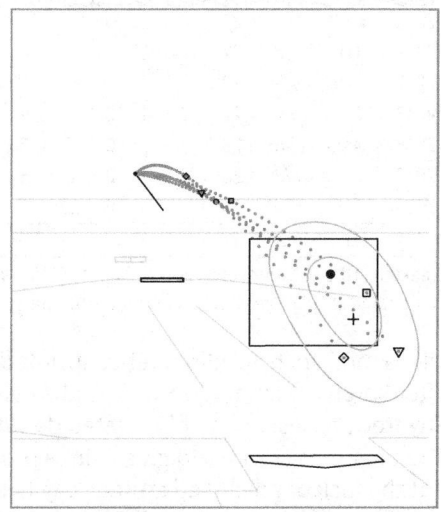

Type	Frequency	Velocity	H Movement	V Movement
● Fastball	36.8%	95 [108]	-6.9 [99]	-12.4 [111]
☐ Sinker	5.4%	94.9 [112]	-13.1 [96]	-17.2 [110]
+ Cutter	10.1%	87.2 [90]	5.2 [119]	-30.9 [71]
▲ Changeup	6.9%	87.5 [109]	-13.6 [88]	-25.9 [104]
✕ Splitter				
▽ Slider	14.1%	82.6 [91]	12.1 [131]	-37.1 [88]
◇ Curveball	26.7%	79.6 [104]	7.8 [100]	-55.6 [83]
✥ Slow Curveball				
✳ Knuckleball				
▼ Screwball				

Shane Bieber RHP

Born: 05/31/95 Age: 24 Bats: R Throws: R
Height: 6'3" Weight: 195 Origin: Round 4, 2016 Draft (#122 overall)

YEAR	TEAM	LVL	AGE	W	L	SV	G	GS	IP	H	HR	BB/9	K/9	K	GB%	BABIP
2016	MHV	A-	21	0	0	0	9	8	24	10	0	0.8	7.9	21	56%	.164
2017	LKC	A	22	2	3	0	5	5	29	34	1	0.3	9.6	31	45%	.375
2017	LYN	A+	22	6	1	0	14	14	90	95	5	0.4	8.2	82	50%	.340
2017	AKR	AA	22	2	1	0	9	9	54^1	56	2	0.8	8.1	49	50%	.331
2018	AKR	AA	23	3	0	0	5	5	31	26	1	0.3	8.7	30	48%	.278
2018	COH	AAA	23	3	1	0	8	8	48^2	30	3	1.1	8.7	47	56%	.225
2018	CLE	MLB	23	11	5	0	20	19	114^2	130	13	1.8	9.3	118	46%	.356
2019	CLE	MLB	24	7	5	0	19	19	100^2	104	14	2.4	8.4	94	45%	.304

Breakout: 18% Improve: 53% Collapse: 12% Attrition: 17% MLB: 83%
Comparables: Luke Weaver, Mike Minor, Drew Smyly

Like a mini Josh Tomlin, Bieber sprinted (definitely didn't walk) to the majors after barely 100 innings above High-A because of an adamant refusal to issue any free passes. In an abbreviated debut, he continued right along that path. The plus-plus command gives him a pretty high floor of capable innings eater, but the lack of advanced stuff or any true out-pitch is what keeps him from topping out as anything more than that. Bieber suddenly missing bats at an elite level would be almost as big of a surprise as making it through an entire comment about Bieber without making a bad reference to the musician with an identical surname.

YEAR	TEAM	LVL	AGE	WHIP	ERA	DRA	WARP	MPH	FB%	WHF	CSP
2016	MHV	A-	21	0.50	0.38	3.40	0.5				
2017	LKC	A	22	1.21	3.10	3.83	0.5				
2017	LYN	A+	22	1.10	3.10	3.30	2.1				
2017	AKR	AA	22	1.12	2.32	3.04	1.4				
2018	AKR	AA	23	0.87	1.16	2.86	0.9				
2018	COH	AAA	23	0.74	1.66	3.26	1.3				
2018	CLE	MLB	23	1.33	4.55	3.32	2.6	94.7	57.4	12.3	51.2
2019	CLE	MLB	24	1.33	3.81	4.33	1.3	94.5	59.1	12.6	52.8

Shane Bieber, continued

Pitch Shape vs LHH

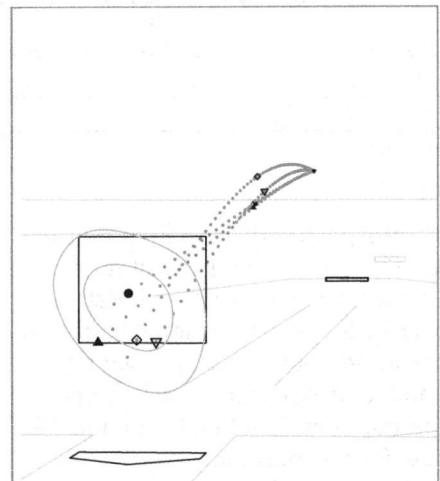

Pitch Shape vs RHH

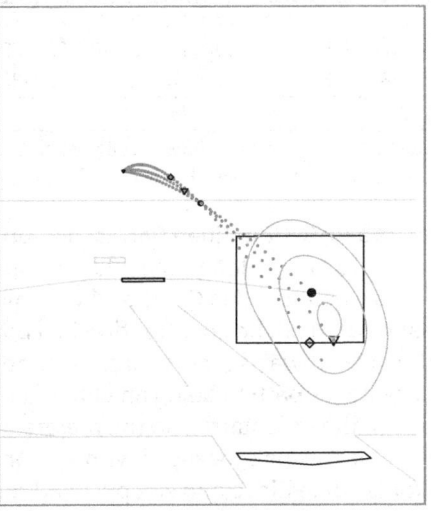

Type	Frequency	Velocity	H Movement	V Movement
● Fastball	57.4%	93.4 [103]	-9.5 [87]	-13.9 [106]
☐ Sinker				
+ Cutter				
▲ Changeup	3.9%	88.1 [111]	-9.8 [108]	-20.7 [120]
✕ Splitter				
▽ Slider	22.7%	84 [98]	2.3 [89]	-34.7 [95]
◇ Curveball	16.0%	80.4 [107]	6.6 [95]	-49.8 [96]
✣ Slow Curveball				
✳ Knuckleball				
▼ Screwball				

Carlos Carrasco RHP

Born: 03/21/87 Age: 32 Bats: R Throws: R
Height: 6'3" Weight: 212 Origin: International Free Agent, 2003

YEAR	TEAM	LVL	AGE	W	L	SV	G	GS	IP	H	HR	BB/9	K/9	K	GB%	BABIP
2016	CLE	MLB	29	11	8	0	25	25	146^1	134	21	2.1	9.2	150	50%	.289
2017	CLE	MLB	30	18	6	0	32	32	200	173	21	2.1	10.2	226	47%	.307
2018	CLE	MLB	31	17	10	0	32	30	192	173	21	2.0	10.8	231	48%	.315
2019	CLE	MLB	32	14	8	0	30	30	180	162	21	2.5	9.8	197	47%	.298

Breakout: 15%   Improve: 33%   Collapse: 30%   Attrition: 6%   MLB: 93%
Comparables: Josh Beckett, Erik Bedard, A.J. Burnett

Years ago, BP identified Carrasco as an elite prospect, with ace potential. Then he was bad for a long time and perhaps was lumped in with the multitude of busts who arrived in Cleveland with him as part of a teardown (think Matt LaPorta). Next, he got attention in a bad way for trying to bean some batters in the head. It was a long, weird, meandering journey, but then he just got right back on his path to being an elite pitcher, and for five seasons now he's been one of the best starters in the majors. He perhaps hasn't gotten the fanfare he deserves, as he's jockeyed with Trevor Bauer for the role of Kluber's Second Fiddle while Cleveland sleepwalked their way to multiple division titles, but a whole lot of teams would be happy to have him as their no. 1. Instead, Carrasco signed a below-market offseason extension that will keep him right where he is.

YEAR	TEAM	LVL	AGE	WHIP	ERA	DRA	WARP	MPH	FB%	WHF	CSP
2016	CLE	MLB	29	1.15	3.32	3.01	3.9	96.8	53.3	13.4	47.1
2017	CLE	MLB	30	1.10	3.29	2.79	6.2	96.3	48.9	14.5	47.5
2018	CLE	MLB	31	1.12	3.38	2.91	5.3	95.6	44.9	16.5	45.9
2019	CLE	MLB	32	1.18	3.16	3.65	3.7	95.1	47.6	15	46.3

Carlos Carrasco, continued

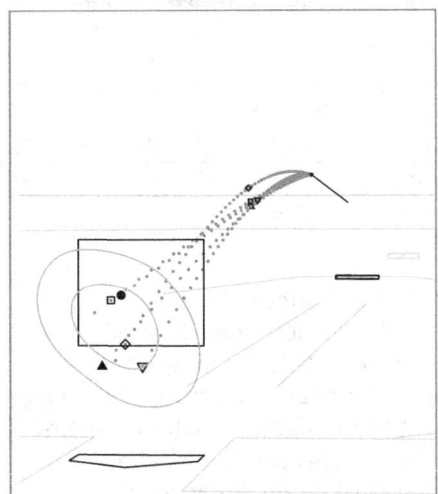
Pitch Shape vs LHH

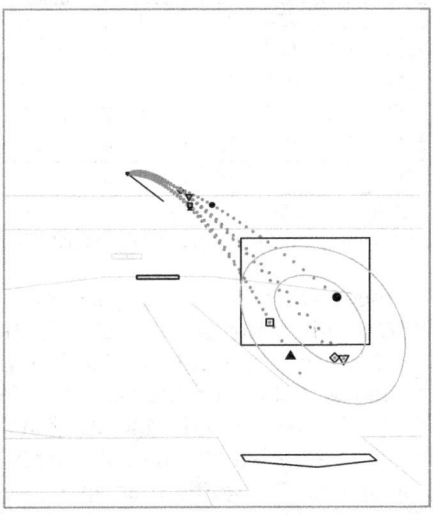
Pitch Shape vs RHH

Type	Frequency	Velocity	H Movement	V Movement
● Fastball	31.3%	94.1 [105]	-9.9 [85]	-15.3 [101]
☐ Sinker	13.6%	93.4 [104]	-14.9 [81]	-21.8 [95]
+ Cutter				
▲ Changeup	16.1%	88.4 [112]	-9 [112]	-31.4 [88]
✕ Splitter				
▽ Slider	29.0%	84.5 [100]	3 [92]	-35.7 [92]
◇ Curveball	10.0%	81.9 [113]	8.3 [102]	-42.3 [113]
⊕ Slow Curveball				
✱ Knuckleball				
▼ Screwball				

Mike Clevinger   RHP

Born: 12/21/90   Age: 28   Bats: R   Throws: R
Height: 6'4"   Weight: 210   Origin: Round 4, 2011 Draft (#135 overall)

YEAR	TEAM	LVL	AGE	W	L	SV	G	GS	IP	H	HR	BB/9	K/9	K	GB%	BABIP
2016	COH	AAA	25	11	1	0	17	17	93	78	8	3.4	9.4	97	40%	.293
2016	CLE	MLB	25	3	3	0	17	10	53	50	8	4.9	8.5	50	40%	.288
2017	COH	AAA	26	3	2	0	7	7	34	28	3	3.7	10.1	38	40%	.298
2017	CLE	MLB	26	12	6	0	27	21	121²	92	13	4.4	10.1	137	40%	.274
2018	CLE	MLB	27	13	8	0	32	32	200	164	21	3.0	9.3	207	41%	.280
2019	CLE	MLB	28	11	8	0	26	26	156	142	21	3.6	9.5	165	40%	.291

Breakout: 11%   Improve: 47%   Collapse: 24%   Attrition: 10%   MLB: 92%
Comparables: Zack Godley, Jacob deGrom, Tyler Thornburg

Clevinger didn't so much break out in 2018 as he continued his breakout of 2017. His pitch mix was basically identical and the results were basically identical. He simply did it for 200 innings instead of 120. The most significant addition was that he added an extra 1.5 miles per hour on his fastball, although oddly his strikeout and walk rates both went down slightly with his newfound velocity. He's a late bloomer like Corey Kluber, but his peripherals show he's more of a no. 2/3 starter than an emergent ace. That said, it's an amazing outcome for a fourth-round pick who was once traded for 20-something innings of Vinnie Pestano.

YEAR	TEAM	LVL	AGE	WHIP	ERA	DRA	WARP	MPH	FB%	WHF	CSP
2016	COH	AAA	25	1.22	3.00	3.12	2.4				
2016	CLE	MLB	25	1.49	5.26	6.15	-0.5	96.1	58.4	10.2	44.9
2017	COH	AAA	26	1.24	2.65	3.80	0.7				
2017	CLE	MLB	26	1.25	3.11	3.61	2.6	94.4	53.5	13.1	42.7
2018	CLE	MLB	27	1.15	3.02	3.52	4.1	95.9	52.9	12.8	48.8
2019	CLE	MLB	28	1.31	3.87	4.41	1.8	94.9	54	12.7	46.1

Mike Clevinger, continued

Pitch Shape vs LHH	Pitch Shape vs RHH
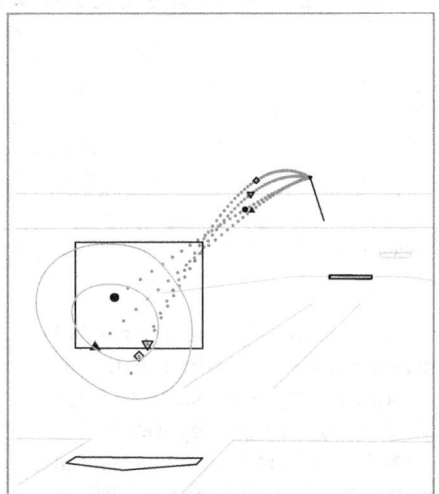	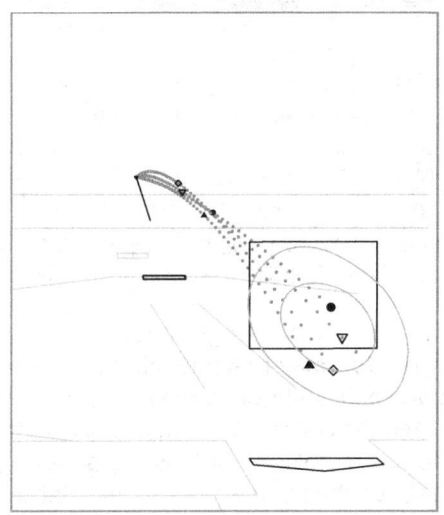

Type	Frequency	Velocity	H Movement	V Movement
● Fastball	52.9%	94.2 [105]	-6.7 [100]	-13 [109]
☐ Sinker				
+ Cutter				
▲ Changeup	14.1%	88.1 [111]	-12.3 [95]	-24.2 [109]
✕ Splitter				
▽ Slider	21.0%	79.9 [80]	15.1 [144]	-36.6 [89]
◇ Curveball	11.9%	75.9 [91]	10.8 [113]	-52 [91]
⊕ Slow Curveball				
✱ Knuckleball				
▼ Screwball				

Tyler Clippard   RHP

Born: 02/14/85   Age: 34   Bats: R   Throws: R
Height: 6'3"   Weight: 200   Origin: Round 9, 2003 Draft (#274 overall)

YEAR	TEAM	LVL	AGE	W	L	SV	G	GS	IP	H	HR	BB/9	K/9	K	GB%	BABIP
2016	ARI	MLB	31	2	3	1	40	0	37^2	34	7	3.6	11.0	46	34%	.310
2016	NYA	MLB	31	2	3	2	29	0	25^1	20	3	3.9	9.2	26	32%	.258
2017	NYA	MLB	32	1	5	1	40	0	36^1	28	7	4.7	10.4	42	35%	.236
2017	CHA	MLB	32	1	1	2	11	0	10	8	0	4.5	10.8	12	30%	.296
2017	HOU	MLB	32	0	2	2	16	0	14	11	3	4.5	11.6	18	36%	.242
2018	TOR	MLB	33	4	3	7	73	1	68^2	57	13	3.0	11.1	85	22%	.272
2019	CLE	MLB	34	3	1	3	53	0	56^2	50	10	3.7	10.2	64	31%	.278

Breakout: 18%   Improve: 35%   Collapse: 34%   Attrition: 14%   MLB: 92%
Comparables: Scott Sauerbeck, Francisco Rodriguez, John Hiller

Inked to a minor-league pact at the start of the season, Clippard wormed his way into a major-league role by late spring and proved an intriguing, if unreliable addition to the Blue Jays' relief corps. He replaced Roberto Osuna when the closer was dealt a 75-game suspension following allegations of domestic violence, but lost it just as quickly to Ryan Tepera and was relegated to mop-up duty in the seventh and eighth for the remainder of the year. While the Blue Jays elected not to give the bespectacled righty an encore in 2019, they provided a platform for him to set a new major league record when, after 10 years and 680 consecutive relief appearances since his previous career start, he opened a game against the Mariners and pitched one disastrous inning of three-hit, two-run, one-strikeout ball.

YEAR	TEAM	LVL	AGE	WHIP	ERA	DRA	WARP	MPH	FB%	WHF	CSP
2016	ARI	MLB	31	1.30	4.30	4.33	0.3	93.3	46.3	13.9	45.8
2016	NYA	MLB	31	1.22	2.49	3.57	0.4	93.8	42.9	13.1	46.6
2017	NYA	MLB	32	1.29	4.95	2.86	0.9	92.3	40.4	15.9	43.9
2017	CHA	MLB	32	1.30	1.80	2.76	0.3	92.8	32.9	14.5	41.2
2017	HOU	MLB	32	1.29	6.43	3.48	0.3	91.6	36.3	12.6	47.3
2018	TOR	MLB	33	1.17	3.67	3.55	1.1	92.3	41.8	15.8	45.5
2019	CLE	MLB	34	1.31	4.68	5.02	0.0	91.5	40.6	14.7	44.6

Tyler Clippard, continued

Pitch Shape vs LHH

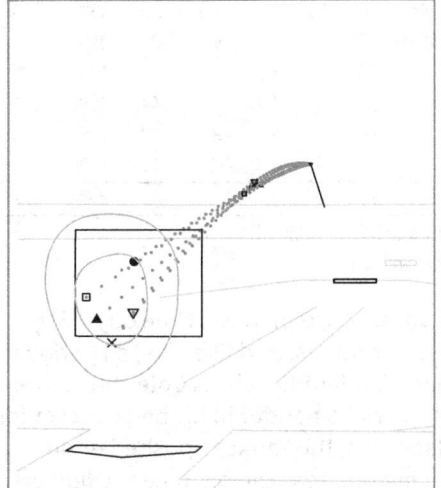

Pitch Shape vs RHH

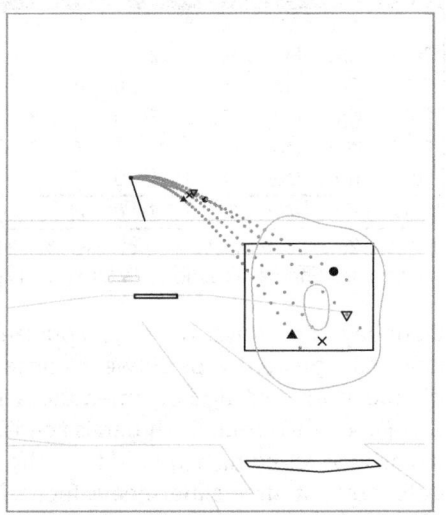

Type	Frequency	Velocity	H Movement	V Movement
● Fastball	35.9%	91.5 [97]	-3.6 [114]	-12.5 [110]
☐ Sinker	5.8%	91.1 [93]	-9.2 [128]	-15.3 [117]
+ Cutter	1.4%	88.5 [99]	0.5 [92]	-18.1 [122]
▲ Changeup	31.4%	79 [75]	-9.9 [107]	-25.2 [106]
✕ Splitter	13.4%	82.5 [83]	-3.1 [120]	-35 [77]
▽ Slider	11.1%	83.6 [96]	2.6 [90]	-31.5 [105]
◇ Curveball	1.0%	75 [87]	7.2 [98]	-48.5 [99]
⊕ Slow Curveball				
✱ Knuckleball				
▼ Screwball				

A.J. Cole   RHP

Born: 01/05/92   Age: 27   Bats: R   Throws: R
Height: 6'5"   Weight: 238   Origin: Round 4, 2010 Draft (#116 overall)

YEAR	TEAM	LVL	AGE	W	L	SV	G	GS	IP	H	HR	BB/9	K/9	K	GB%	BABIP
2016	SYR	AAA	24	8	8	0	22	22	124²	131	16	2.5	7.9	109	43%	.310
2016	WAS	MLB	24	1	2	0	8	8	38¹	37	7	3.3	9.2	39	32%	.283
2017	SYR	AAA	25	4	5	0	18	18	93¹	127	7	3.5	7.6	79	42%	.390
2017	WAS	MLB	25	3	5	0	11	8	52	51	8	4.7	7.6	44	45%	.293
2018	WAS	MLB	26	1	1	0	4	2	10¹	16	6	5.2	8.7	10	27%	.323
2018	NYA	MLB	26	3	1	0	28	0	38	39	9	3.8	11.6	49	37%	.319
2019	CLE	MLB	27	1	1	0	14	0	14	13	2	3.7	9.9	16	39%	.297

Breakout: 26%   Improve: 50%   Collapse: 5%   Attrition: 13%   MLB: 68%
Comparables: Christian Friedrich, Billy Buckner, Chase Anderson

Eight days. Five days. Ten days. Fourteen days. Fourteen days. Nine days. Five days. All represent gaps between consecutive outings, and likewise, all periods of time where fans and commentators alike wondered... why is Cole still on the 25-man roster? Brian Cashman is keeping the right-hander in his back pocket for a reason. After being acquired from the Nationals, the Yankees pushed upon Cole their patented slider-heavy focus, having him toss the pitch nearly *half* of the time. It seemed successful at first, generating whiffs on nearly a third of sliders in June, but it then declined month after month. That being said, overall, Cole had the third-highest swinging strike rate on the team, and when you combine a mid-90s fastball with that slider, you get the ingredients for a successful relief ace. His lack of opportunity, then, could be more of a symptom of one of the deepest bullpens in baseball than pure ability. Whether he remains with the team and stays a decent last option, or moves on to another and becomes something more like a middle reliever or a 7th inning guy, he will get a chance to prove his merit in a more consistent manner.

YEAR	TEAM	LVL	AGE	WHIP	ERA	DRA	WARP	MPH	FB%	WHF	CSP
2016	SYR	AAA	24	1.33	4.26	3.89	2.1				
2016	WAS	MLB	24	1.33	5.17	4.92	0.2	93.4	57.3	10.9	44
2017	SYR	AAA	25	1.75	5.88	4.60	1.1				
2017	WAS	MLB	25	1.50	3.81	4.53	0.6	95.1	54.8	10.9	45.7
2018	WAS	MLB	26	2.13	13.06	7.82	-0.3	94.2	44.1	7.3	49.1
2018	NYA	MLB	26	1.45	4.26	2.88	0.9	95.7	30.9	16.9	43.2
2019	CLE	MLB	27	1.33	3.51	4.07	0.2	94.4	46.7	12.8	45.3

A.J. Cole, continued

Pitch Shape vs LHH

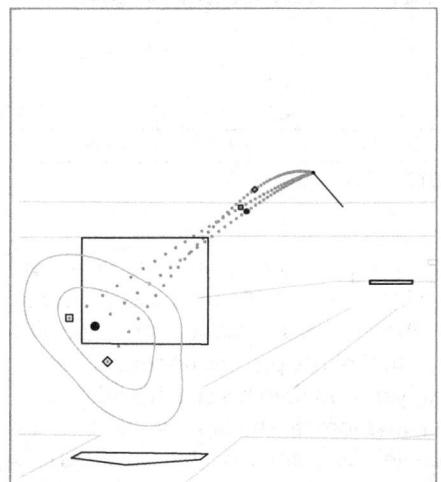

Pitch Shape vs RHH

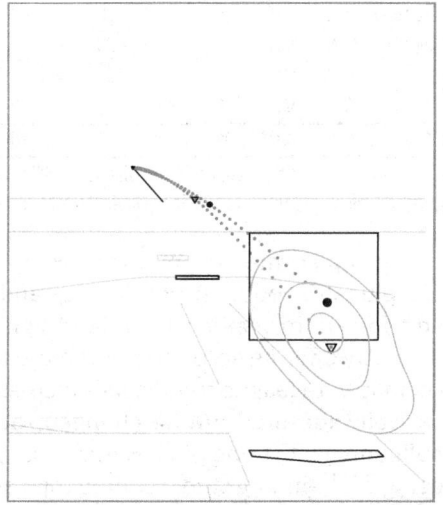

Type	Frequency	Velocity	H Movement	V Movement
● Fastball	25.4%	94 [105]	-7.2 [97]	-13.9 [106]
□ Sinker	8.2%	92.9 [102]	-12.2 [103]	-16.8 [112]
+ Cutter				
▲ Changeup	2.7%	87 [107]	-14.3 [84]	-25.3 [106]
× Splitter				
▽ Slider	43.5%	84.6 [101]	1.3 [85]	-29.2 [111]
◇ Curveball	20.1%	79.8 [105]	3.4 [81]	-38.8 [121]
⊕ Slow Curveball				
✳ Knuckleball				
▼ Screwball				

Cleveland Indians 2019

Brad Hand LHP
Born: 03/20/90 Age: 29 Bats: L Throws: L
Height: 6'3" Weight: 228 Origin: Round 2, 2008 Draft (#52 overall)

YEAR	TEAM	LVL	AGE	W	L	SV	G	GS	IP	H	HR	BB/9	K/9	K	GB%	BABIP
2016	SDN	MLB	26	4	4	1	82	0	89[1]	63	8	3.6	11.2	111	47%	.264
2017	SDN	MLB	27	3	4	21	72	0	79[1]	54	9	2.3	11.8	104	46%	.263
2018	SDN	MLB	28	2	4	24	41	0	44[1]	33	5	3.0	13.2	65	48%	.298
2018	CLE	MLB	28	0	1	8	28	0	27[2]	19	3	4.2	13.3	41	44%	.286
2019	CLE	MLB	29	3	2	35	51	0	53	40	4	3.5	11.8	70	45%	.290

Breakout: 23% Improve: 48% Collapse: 28% Attrition: 11% MLB: 99%
Comparables: Justin Grimm, Mark Davis, Drew Storen

Once a replacement-level starter, Hand has now posted three straight years with 100-plus strikeouts, 70-plus innings and an ERA below 3.00 out of the bullpen. And, for a third year in a row, Hand significantly increased his slider usage, with the nasty offering accounting for more than half of the pitches he threw. In keeping with league trends, he's increasingly mothballed his sinker and basically doesn't throw his changeup at all anymore. In the land of the bullpenning, the one pitch Hand is king. Cleveland made a big bet on Hand being a late-inning stud, sending top catching prospect Francisco Mejia to San Diego for him at midseason.

YEAR	TEAM	LVL	AGE	WHIP	ERA	DRA	WARP	MPH	FB%	WHF	CSP
2016	SDN	MLB	26	1.11	2.92	3.58	1.4	95.6	61.1	12.9	46
2017	SDN	MLB	27	0.93	2.16	3.03	1.9	95.0	51.1	14.1	46.1
2018	SDN	MLB	28	1.08	3.05	3.15	0.9	95.9	44.2	13.6	50
2018	CLE	MLB	28	1.16	2.28	3.47	0.5	95.6	48.1	13.2	52.7
2019	CLE	MLB	29	1.13	2.46	3.09	1.3	94.8	51.9	13.5	48.1

Brad Hand, continued

Pitch Shape vs LHH

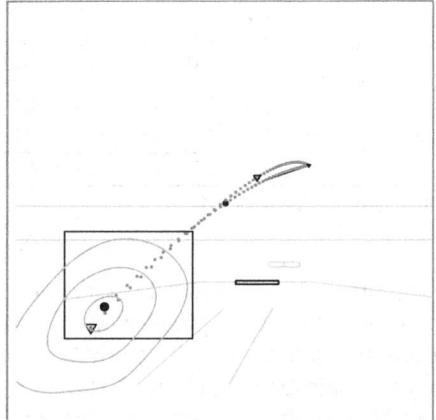

Pitch Shape vs RHH

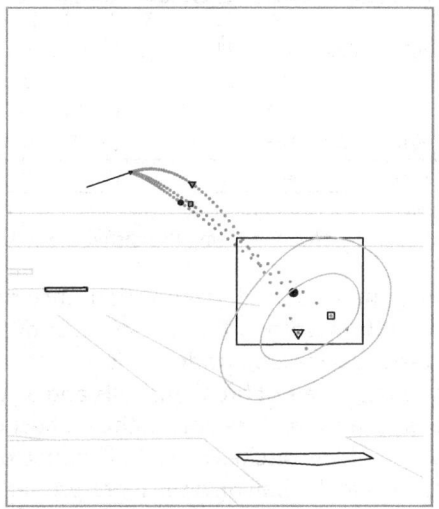

Type	Frequency	Velocity	H Movement	V Movement
● Fastball	29.9%	94.1 [105]	9.2 [88]	-15.1 [102]
☐ Sinker	15.8%	93.8 [106]	14.4 [85]	-23.7 [89]
+ Cutter				
▲ Changeup				
✕ Splitter				
▽ Slider	54.3%	82.3 [90]	-14.3 [141]	-40.8 [77]
◇ Curveball				
⊕ Slow Curveball				
✱ Knuckleball				
▼ Screwball				

Chih-Wei Hu RHP

Born: 11/04/93 Age: 25 Bats: R Throws: R
Height: 6'0" Weight: 220 Origin: International Free Agent, 2012

YEAR	TEAM	LVL	AGE	W	L	SV	G	GS	IP	H	HR	BB/9	K/9	K	GB%	BABIP
2016	MNT	AA	22	7	8	0	24	24	142^2	128	7	2.3	6.8	107	44%	.283
2017	DUR	AAA	23	4	1	2	31	4	61^2	59	9	1.8	8.3	57	46%	.292
2017	TBA	MLB	23	1	1	0	6	0	10	5	2	3.6	8.1	9	37%	.120
2018	DUR	AAA	24	5	7	0	24	19	102^1	113	14	2.5	8.1	92	38%	.321
2018	TBA	MLB	24	0	0	0	5	0	13	7	2	2.1	8.3	12	23%	.152
2019	CLE	MLB	25	1	1	0	23	0	24^1	23	4	3.0	8.5	23	40%	.290

Breakout: 7% Improve: 19% Collapse: 17% Attrition: 33% MLB: 48%
Comparables: Trevor Williams, Rob Zastryzny, Eric Jokisch

Hu joined his third organization since turning pro at age 18 out of Taiwan, going from Minnesota to Tampa Bay and now to Cleveland following a 40-man-clearing offseason trade. Hu is a pitcher more than a thrower, with a low-90s fastball, a pair of breaking balls and a very good palmball. The latter has the best chance to miss bats at the highest level. He has above-average navigation, although his pitches can go off course once in the zone and his lack of height can leave the ball on a tee if not properly executed. He's worked mostly as a starter, although all 11 of his big-league appearances have come in relief.

YEAR	TEAM	LVL	AGE	WHIP	ERA	DRA	WARP	MPH	FB%	WHF	CSP
2016	MNT	AA	22	1.15	2.59	3.31	3.1				
2017	DUR	AAA	23	1.15	3.06	3.55	1.3				
2017	TBA	MLB	23	0.90	2.70	5.64	-0.1	95.2	59.9	14.4	39
2018	DUR	AAA	24	1.38	4.66	4.20	1.5				
2018	TBA	MLB	24	0.77	4.15	4.27	0.1	94.7	47.7	10.8	50.6
2019	CLE	MLB	25	1.28	4.10	4.57	0.2	94.6	53.9	12.5	46.5

Chih-Wei Hu, continued

Pitch Shape vs LHH

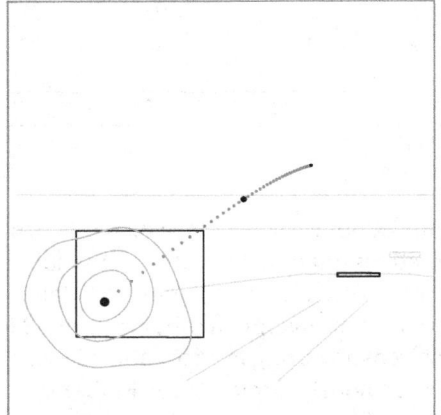

Pitch Shape vs RHH

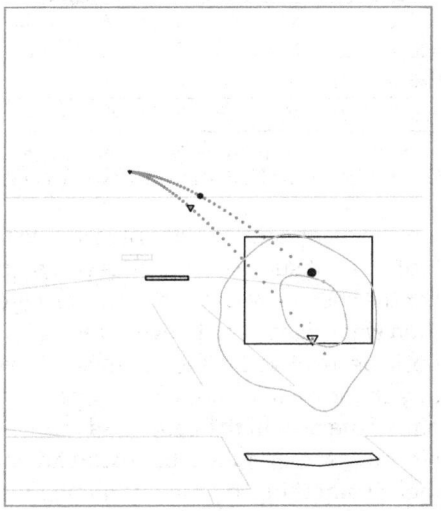

Type		Frequency	Velocity	H Movement	V Movement
●	Fastball	41.5%	93 [102]	-3.8 [113]	-14.4 [104]
☐	Sinker	6.2%	93.6 [106]	-13 [96]	-17.4 [110]
+	Cutter				
▲	Changeup	24.6%	87.7 [110]	-11.5 [99]	-29.7 [93]
✕	Splitter				
▽	Slider	20.0%	88.3 [117]	1.9 [87]	-24.2 [126]
◇	Curveball	7.7%	79.4 [104]	2.4 [77]	-41.9 [114]
⊕	Slow Curveball				
✳	Knuckleball				
▼	Screwball				

Corey Kluber   RHP

Born: 04/10/86   Age: 33   Bats: R   Throws: R
Height: 6'4"   Weight: 215   Origin: Round 4, 2007 Draft (#134 overall)

YEAR	TEAM	LVL	AGE	W	L	SV	G	GS	IP	H	HR	BB/9	K/9	K	GB%	BABIP
2016	CLE	MLB	30	18	9	0	32	32	215	170	22	2.4	9.5	227	46%	.271
2017	CLE	MLB	31	18	4	0	29	29	203²	141	21	1.6	11.7	265	46%	.267
2018	CLE	MLB	32	20	7	0	33	33	215	179	25	1.4	9.3	222	46%	.276
2019	CLE	MLB	33	15	8	0	29	29	194¹	176	24	2.3	9.2	198	45%	.291

Breakout: 12%   Improve: 40%   Collapse: 22%   Attrition: 14%   MLB: 97%
Comparables: Pedro Martinez, Tom Seaver, Adam Wainwright

Another year, another 200-plus innings with 220-plus strikeouts, which marks a fifth straight such season since he completed his full transformation into Klubot. For the second year in a row, he struggled at one point with a minor injury and then went right back to eviscerating hitters with his five-pitch mix. He turns 33 in April, he just had his second miserable postseason outing in a row and he lost a tiny shade off his four-seam fastball. This is obviously nitpicking, as Kluber is one of the best in the game and is an excellent bet to remain so. He did throw his four-seamer quite a bit less in favor of more cutters and sinkers, which might mean something, or it might mean Kluber is a smug jerk with way too many excellent pitches and he can use them as much or as little as he likes.

YEAR	TEAM	LVL	AGE	WHIP	ERA	DRA	WARP	MPH	FB%	WHF	CSP
2016	CLE	MLB	30	1.06	3.14	3.33	5.0	94.8	51.2	13.7	46.1
2017	CLE	MLB	31	0.87	2.25	2.28	7.5	94.0	42.4	16.4	47.2
2018	CLE	MLB	32	0.99	2.89	2.84	6.1	93.4	41.6	13	46.4
2019	CLE	MLB	33	1.15	3.34	3.84	3.6	92.9	43.8	14.1	46

Corey Kluber, continued

Pitch Shape vs LHH

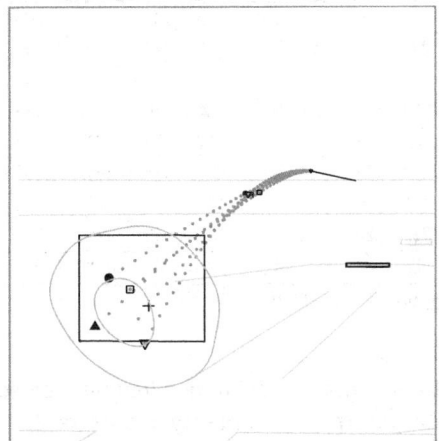

Pitch Shape vs RHH

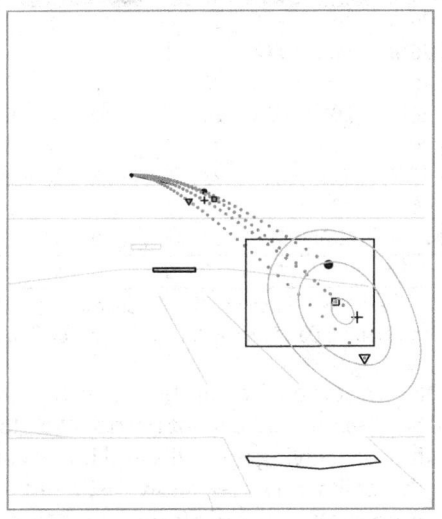

Type	Frequency	Velocity	H Movement	V Movement
● Fastball	9.1%	92.4 [100]	-5.5 [106]	-15.7 [100]
□ Sinker	32.6%	92.4 [100]	-13.1 [96]	-21.8 [95]
+ Cutter	29.3%	88.9 [101]	3.2 [108]	-25.5 [93]
▲ Changeup	6.6%	85.6 [101]	-10.5 [104]	-29.9 [92]
✕ Splitter				
▽ Slider	22.5%	84.2 [99]	13.7 [138]	-32.8 [101]
◇ Curveball				
✢ Slow Curveball				
✱ Knuckleball				
▼ Screwball				

Indians Player Analysis

Cleveland Indians 2019

Tyler Olson LHP
Born: 10/02/89   Age: 29   Bats: R   Throws: L
Height: 6'3"   Weight: 195   Origin: Round 7, 2013 Draft (#207 overall)

YEAR	TEAM	LVL	AGE	W	L	SV	G	GS	IP	H	HR	BB/9	K/9	K	GB%	BABIP
2016	NYA	MLB	26	0	0	0	1	0	2^2	3	0	6.8	0.0	0	27%	.273
2016	SWB	AAA	26	1	2	0	11	3	27^1	31	2	2.6	6.9	21	53%	.341
2016	OMA	AAA	26	0	0	0	5	0	6^1	10	1	2.8	2.8	2	48%	.346
2016	COH	AAA	26	1	0	0	9	0	10^2	12	1	5.1	8.4	10	29%	.333
2017	COH	AAA	27	2	0	2	34	0	42	28	7	2.6	11.6	54	43%	.241
2017	CLE	MLB	27	1	0	1	30	0	20	13	0	2.7	8.1	18	54%	.250
2018	COH	AAA	28	2	1	1	17	0	12^1	8	0	2.2	13.1	18	42%	.308
2018	CLE	MLB	28	2	1	0	43	0	27^1	26	4	4.0	13.2	40	42%	.355
2019	CLE	MLB	29	3	2	0	51	0	53	46	6	4.0	10.7	63	43%	.299

Breakout: 15%   Improve: 22%   Collapse: 26%   Attrition: 25%   MLB: 59%
Comparables: Darin Downs, Simon Castro, Rob Scahill

Olson's composite numbers in 2018 numbers — his longest major-league look so far — are mediocre if not horrid. At a glance, he strikes out plenty of batters while also giving up walks and home runs at an unacceptable rate. A quick look at his splits, however, show Olson did not really change, he was just misused. As a pure LOOGY, he did his job pretty well, limiting lefties to a .182/.250/.345 line. But for some reason he faced as many right-handed batters (58) as he did lefties (60), and they hit like prime Albert Belle against him. Somewhere Randy Williams is weeping.

YEAR	TEAM	LVL	AGE	WHIP	ERA	DRA	WARP	MPH	FB%	WHF	CSP
2016	NYA	MLB	26	1.88	6.75	7.53	-0.1	90.1	70.2	12.8	46.6
2016	SWB	AAA	26	1.43	5.27	4.81	0.1				
2016	OMA	AAA	26	1.89	2.84	4.44	0.0				
2016	COH	AAA	26	1.69	5.91	3.68	0.2				
2017	COH	AAA	27	0.95	3.21	2.81	1.1				
2017	CLE	MLB	27	0.95	0.00	3.90	0.3	90.3	39.8	10.7	49.2
2018	COH	AAA	28	0.89	3.65	2.61	0.4				
2018	CLE	MLB	28	1.39	4.94	2.74	0.7	90.2	47.6	15.3	45.5
2019	CLE	MLB	29	1.30	3.26	3.86	0.8	89.6	45.9	13.7	47

Tyler Olson, continued

Pitch Shape vs LHH

Pitch Shape vs RHH

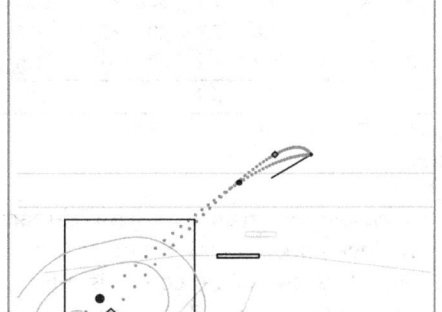
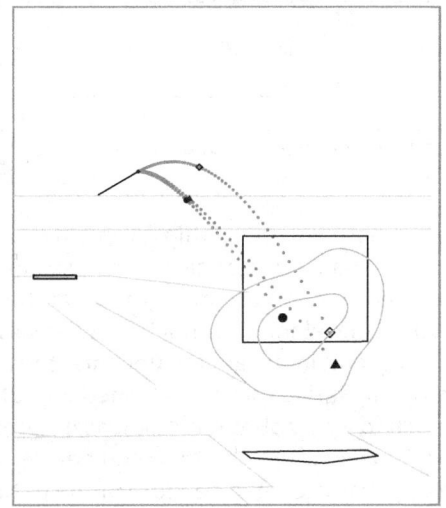

Type	Frequency	Velocity	H Movement	V Movement
● Fastball	43.6%	89 [89]	0.5 [129]	-23.7 [75]
☐ Sinker	4.0%	89.8 [87]	11.9 [106]	-28.2 [74]
+ Cutter				
▲ Changeup	14.6%	84.9 [98]	8.4 [115]	-33.6 [82]
✕ Splitter				
▽ Slider				
◇ Curveball	37.8%	74.6 [86]	-17.1 [139]	-49.3 [97]
⊕ Slow Curveball				
✳ Knuckleball				
▼ Screwball				

Dan Otero   RHP

Born: 02/19/85   Age: 34   Bats: R   Throws: R
Height: 6'3"   Weight: 205   Origin: Round 21, 2007 Draft (#644 overall)

YEAR	TEAM	LVL	AGE	W	L	SV	G	GS	IP	H	HR	BB/9	K/9	K	GB%	BABIP
2016	CLE	MLB	31	5	1	1	62	0	70²	54	2	1.3	7.3	57	64%	.260
2017	CLE	MLB	32	3	0	0	52	0	60	63	6	1.4	5.7	38	65%	.302
2018	CLE	MLB	33	2	1	1	61	0	58²	69	12	0.8	6.6	43	61%	.310
2019	CLE	MLB	34	2	1	0	32	0	34	35	4	2.7	6.8	26	57%	.297

Breakout: 19%   Improve: 35%   Collapse: 30%   Attrition: 9%   MLB: 85%
Comparables: Paul Quantrill, Mark Eichhorn, Doug Jones

Otero has been many things: an old rookie, a waiver wire transient, a multi-team journeyman. And, for his first two seasons in Cleveland, a below-the-radar bullpen asset on the strength of a ground-ball rate above 60 percent. His third year in Cleveland was much rougher, as his strand rate dropped, a few more balls got hit in the air and uncharacteristically he allowed a boatload of home runs. His surface statistics turned out rather ugly as a result. DRA says it wasn't much to worry about, though, as his ground-ball rate was still excellent and he walked even fewer batters than before. However, as a high-contact sinker-baller, he's always going to be more prone to the whims of fortune than the flamethrowers of the world.

YEAR	TEAM	LVL	AGE	WHIP	ERA	DRA	WARP	MPH	FB%	WHF	CSP
2016	CLE	MLB	31	0.91	1.53	3.86	0.9	92.9	78.2	8.2	49.5
2017	CLE	MLB	32	1.20	2.85	4.46	0.5	91.6	80.3	8.2	51.4
2018	CLE	MLB	33	1.26	5.22	4.26	0.4	91.5	79.7	9.1	49.2
2019	CLE	MLB	34	1.33	3.95	4.43	0.3	90.8	78.3	8.5	49.2

Dan Otero, continued

Pitch Shape vs LHH

Pitch Shape vs RHH

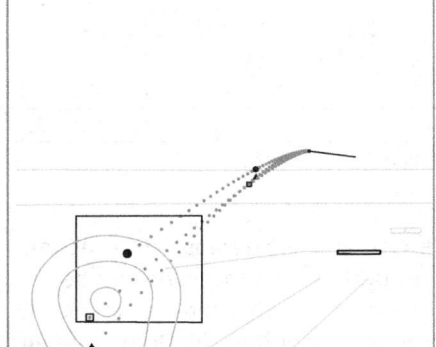
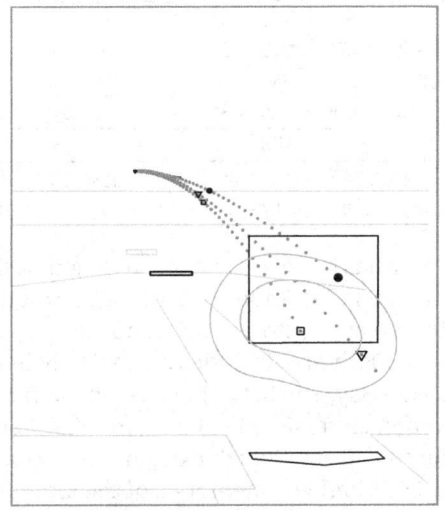

Type	Frequency	Velocity	H Movement	V Movement
● Fastball	12.4%	90.6 [94]	-8 [94]	-17.2 [95]
☐ Sinker	67.4%	90.5 [90]	-14.9 [81]	-24.3 [87]
+ Cutter				
▲ Changeup	12.7%	83.1 [91]	-11.3 [100]	-34.4 [79]
✕ Splitter				
▽ Slider	7.6%	81.9 [89]	3.4 [94]	-35.9 [91]
◇ Curveball				
⊕ Slow Curveball				
✳ Knuckleball				
▼ Screwball				

Oliver Perez LHP

Born: 08/15/81 Age: 37 Bats: L Throws: L
Height: 6'3" Weight: 225 Origin: International Free Agent, 1999

YEAR	TEAM	LVL	AGE	W	L	SV	G	GS	IP	H	HR	BB/9	K/9	K	GB%	BABIP
2016	WAS	MLB	34	2	3	0	64	0	40	38	4	4.5	10.4	46	43%	.324
2017	WAS	MLB	35	0	0	1	50	0	33	32	4	3.3	10.6	39	32%	.333
2018	SWB	AAA	36	1	0	0	16	0	14	17	1	1.9	9.6	15	33%	.421
2018	CLE	MLB	36	1	1	0	51	0	32¹	17	1	1.9	12.0	43	46%	.239
2019	CLE	MLB	37	2	1	0	28	0	29	26	4	4.0	10.3	34	41%	.301

Breakout: 24% Improve: 42% Collapse: 25% Attrition: 6% MLB: 86%
Comparables: Scott Eyre, Trever Miller, Kyle Farnsworth

Perez has been around for so long that the list of players he was in transactions with includes Roberto Hernandez. Not the Roberto Hernandez who was better known as Fausto Carmona, but the guy who closed for the White Sox in the mid-90s. It also includes Xavier Nady (remember Xavier Nady?!), Brian Giles and Jason Bay. The list of players who appeared in Perez's first career game includes Ruben Sierra, Ray Lankford, Ron Gant and a Jamie Moyer, who hadn't even turned 40 yet. Perez's existence as a competent part of a major-league bullpen in 2018 harkens memories of the famous quote from the cinematic masterpiece, *The Sandlot*: "Heroes get remembered, but lefties never die."

YEAR	TEAM	LVL	AGE	WHIP	ERA	DRA	WARP	MPH	FB%	WHF	CSP
2016	WAS	MLB	34	1.45	4.95	4.68	0.1	94.3	57.3	9.9	50.3
2017	WAS	MLB	35	1.33	4.64	6.18	-0.4	94.6	57.3	11	53.6
2018	SWB	AAA	36	1.43	2.57	3.09	0.3				
2018	CLE	MLB	36	0.74	1.39	2.61	0.9	93.9	50.9	16	52.2
2019	CLE	MLB	37	1.37	3.77	4.29	0.3	92.8	53.8	12.1	50.9

Oliver Perez, continued

Pitch Shape vs LHH

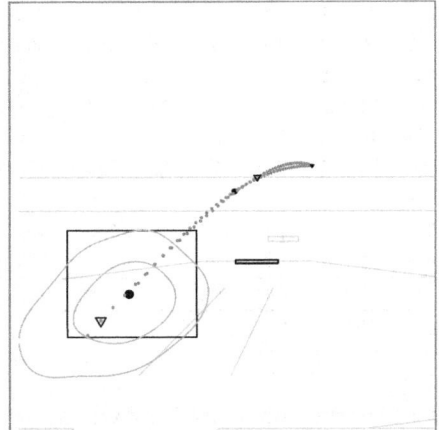

Pitch Shape vs RHH

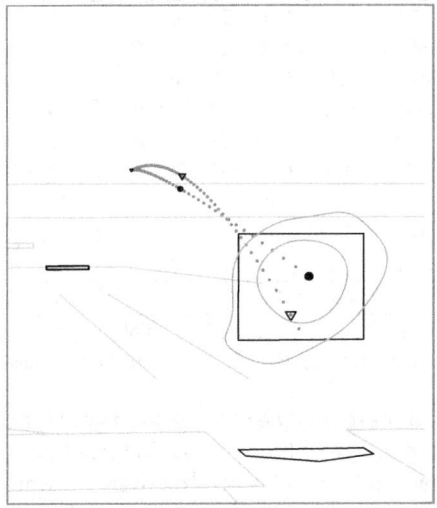

Type	Frequency	Velocity	H Movement	V Movement
● Fastball	47.0%	92.1 [99]	14.7 [63]	-20.5 [85]
□ Sinker	3.8%	91.6 [95]	15.5 [76]	-23.3 [90]
+ Cutter				
▲ Changeup	0.2%	87.6 [109]	15.2 [79]	-24.5 [108]
× Splitter				
▽ Slider	48.9%	79 [76]	-7 [109]	-39.7 [80]
◇ Curveball				
⊕ Slow Curveball				
✳ Knuckleball				
▼ Screwball				

Cleveland Indians 2019

Neil Ramirez   RHP
Born: 05/25/89   Age: 30   Bats: R   Throws: R
Height: 6'4"   Weight: 215   Origin: Round 1, 2007 Draft (#44 overall)

YEAR	TEAM	LVL	AGE	W	L	SV	G	GS	IP	H	HR	BB/9	K/9	K	GB%	BABIP
2016	CHN	MLB	27	0	0	0	8	0	7^2	5	1	9.4	11.7	10	29%	.250
2016	MIL	MLB	27	0	0	0	2	0	1^2	2	2	0.0	16.2	3	25%	.000
2016	MIN	MLB	27	0	0	0	8	0	14^2	15	5	6.1	6.8	11	25%	.256
2016	ROC	AAA	27	0	0	0	16	0	20^1	14	2	3.1	12.0	27	26%	.267
2017	SFN	MLB	28	0	0	0	9	0	10^1	15	2	3.5	15.7	18	27%	.464
2017	NYN	MLB	28	0	1	0	20	0	21	20	4	7.3	11.1	26	33%	.302
2017	SYR	AAA	28	2	1	1	14	0	14^2	23	3	4.9	12.3	20	33%	.465
2018	COH	AAA	29	2	1	3	14	0	18^2	16	4	1.4	15.4	32	13%	.353
2018	CLE	MLB	29	0	3	0	47	0	41^2	36	9	3.9	11.0	51	36%	.273
2019	CLE	MLB	30	1	1	0	18	0	19	18	3	4.4	10.8	23	34%	.297

Breakout: 19%   Improve: 37%   Collapse: 27%   Attrition: 19%   MLB: 86%
Comparables: J.J. Hoover, Mike Dunn, Boone Logan

Did there really exist any such goal for this wandering mankind? That was a question to which he would have liked an answer before it was too late. Moses had not been allowed to enter the land of promise either. But he had been allowed to see it, from the top of the mountain, spread at his feet. Thus, it was easy to die, with the visible certainty of one's goal before one's eyes. He, Neil Andrew Ramirez, had not been taken to the top of a mountain; and wherever his eye looked, he saw nothing but waivers and the darkness of Triple-A. A dull blow struck the back of his slider. He had long expected it and yet it took him unawares. He felt, wondering, his knees give way and his body whirl round in a half-turn. How theatrical, he thought as he spun, and yet I feel nothing. He stood, gazing up on the mound, with his cheek on the cool glove leather. It got dark, the sea carried him rocking on its nocturnal surface. Walks passed through him, like streaks of mist over the water. Outside, someone was knocking on the clubhouse door, he dreamed that they were coming to release him; but on what team was he? He made an effort to slip his arm into his ice-compress sleeve. But whose color-print logo was hanging over his locker and looking at him? Was it the GM or was it the reporter — with the sympathetic smile or he with the same questions? A shapeless figure bent over him, he smelt the fresh leather of the iPhone case recording in front of him; but what insignia did his opponent wear on the sleeves and shoulder straps of his uniform? And in whose name did it raise the dark bat barrel? A second, smashing blow hit his belt-high four-seam. Then all became quiet. There was the sea again with its sounds. A wave slowly lifted him up. It came from afar and traveled sedately on, a shrug of eternity.

YEAR	TEAM	LVL	AGE	WHIP	ERA	DRA	WARP	MPH	FB%	WHF	CSP
2016	CHN	MLB	27	1.70	4.70	4.09	0.1	94.3	50.7	13.2	44
2016	MIL	MLB	27	1.20	10.80	1.49	0.1	94.1	76	24	42.1
2016	MIN	MLB	27	1.70	6.14	5.76	-0.1	94.5	61.2	11.6	47.9
2016	ROC	AAA	27	1.03	3.10	3.08	0.4				
2017	SFN	MLB	28	1.84	8.71	3.73	0.2	94.6	55.9	12.6	42.3
2017	NYN	MLB	28	1.76	6.43	3.74	0.3	94.9	44.5	13.2	45
2017	SYR	AAA	28	2.11	6.14	3.55	0.3				
2018	COH	AAA	29	1.02	3.38	2.38	0.6				
2018	CLE	MLB	29	1.30	4.54	3.64	0.6	96.8	57.1	16.3	47.5
2019	*CLE*	*MLB*	*30*	*1.40*	*4.21*	*4.66*	*0.1*	*95.0*	*54.4*	*14.5*	*45.9*

Cleveland Indians 2019

Neil Ramirez, continued

Pitch Shape vs LHH
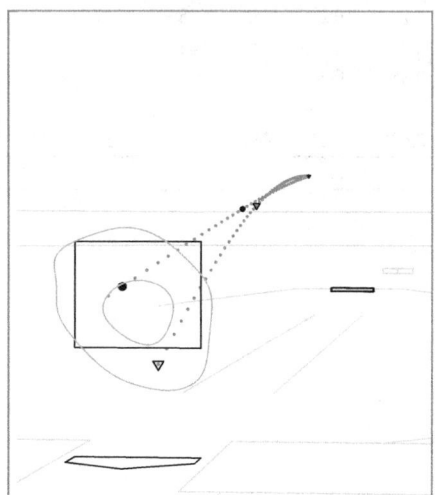

Pitch Shape vs RHH
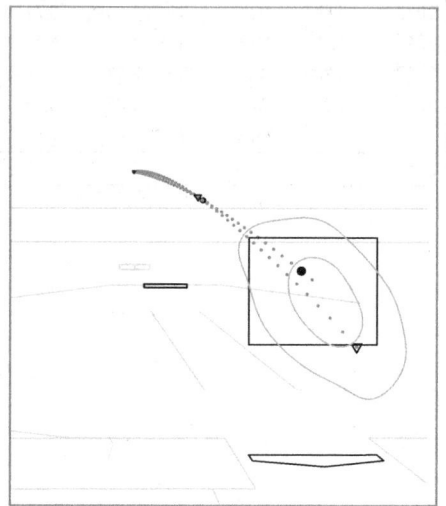

Type	Frequency	Velocity	H Movement	V Movement
● Fastball	57.1%	95.7 [110]	-5.8 [104]	-10.7 [116]
☐ Sinker				
+ Cutter				
▲ Changeup	0.3%	92.9 [130]	-11.9 [97]	-23.8 [110]
✕ Splitter				
▽ Slider	42.6%	86.2 [108]	5.7 [103]	-32 [103]
◇ Curveball				
⊕ Slow Curveball				
✳ Knuckleball				
▼ Screwball				

Alex Wilson   RHP

Born: 11/03/86   Age: 32   Bats: R   Throws: R
Height: 6'0"   Weight: 227   Origin: Round 2, 2009 Draft (#77 overall)

YEAR	TEAM	LVL	AGE	W	L	SV	G	GS	IP	H	HR	BB/9	K/9	K	GB%	BABIP
2016	DET	MLB	29	4	0	0	62	0	73	68	5	2.6	6.0	49	45%	.285
2017	DET	MLB	30	2	5	2	66	0	60	67	7	2.2	6.3	42	42%	.311
2018	DET	MLB	31	2	4	0	59	0	61^2	50	8	2.2	6.3	43	50%	.237
2019	CLE	MLB	32	2	1	1	48	0	50^1	50	7	3.3	7.0	39	45%	.289

Breakout: 22%   Improve: 42%   Collapse: 29%   Attrition: 18%   MLB: 86%
Comparables: Burke Badenhop, Jared Hughes, Geoff Geary

Making a living as a relief pitcher can be exhausting, especially since 649 different players made relief appearances last year. Take away about 100 that were swingmen or position players, and we're still left with about 17 different true relievers per team. Try naming them all. Some stand out with a crazy good breaking pitch. Some ramp up the velocity. Some are Carter Capps and do a weird delivery so they can go viral. Alex Wilson does none of this. He chooses to remain in the background. He's a flatly dull pitcher who doesn't strike out many batters, but limits baserunners across multiple innings. He's done this for four years and counting. The only thing he's done to stand out is sort of resemble Chris Pratt and become the only MLB pitcher born in Saudi Arabia, but those are really things his *parents* did.

YEAR	TEAM	LVL	AGE	WHIP	ERA	DRA	WARP	MPH	FB%	WHF	CSP
2016	DET	MLB	29	1.22	2.96	5.20	-0.2	93.9	56.1	9.8	43
2017	DET	MLB	30	1.37	4.50	5.48	-0.2	94.0	58.3	9.5	46.7
2018	DET	MLB	31	1.05	3.36	4.10	0.6	93.2	41.9	9.7	41.6
2019	CLE	MLB	32	1.37	4.62	4.93	0.1	92.7	50.7	9.6	43.3

Alex Wilson, continued

Pitch Shape vs LHH

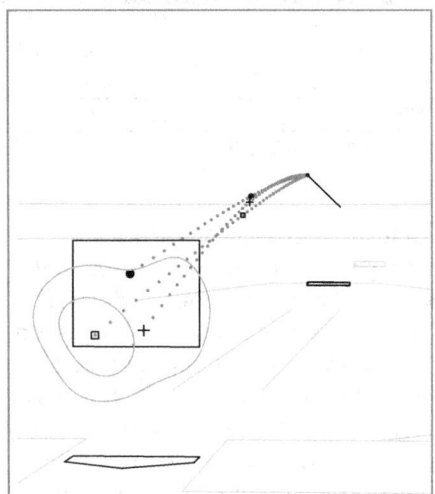

Pitch Shape vs RHH

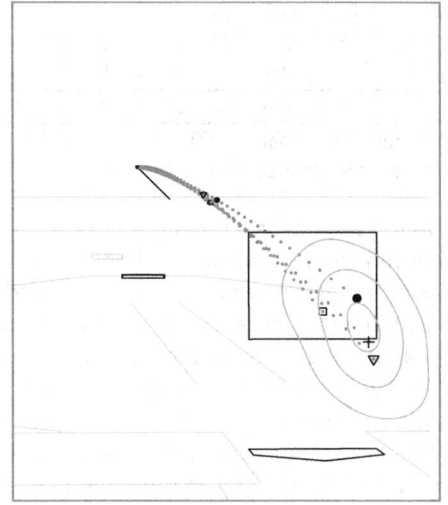

Type	Frequency	Velocity	H Movement	V Movement
● Fastball	18.3%	92.7 [101]	-4.5 [110]	-13.6 [107]
☐ Sinker	23.5%	92.6 [101]	-10 [121]	-16.3 [113]
+ Cutter	49.9%	87.1 [90]	4.9 [118]	-26.5 [89]
▲ Changeup	1.8%	89.1 [115]	-11.7 [98]	-22.1 [116]
✕ Splitter				
▽ Slider	6.4%	84.3 [99]	5.5 [103]	-33.6 [98]
◇ Curveball				
⊕ Slow Curveball				
✳ Knuckleball				
▼ Screwball				

Will Benson   RF

Born: 06/16/98   Age: 21   Bats: L   Throws: L
Height: 6'5"   Weight: 225   Origin: Round 1, 2016 Draft (#14 overall)

YEAR	TEAM	LVL	AGE	PA	R	2B	3B	HR	RBI	BB	K	SB	CS	AVG/OBP/SLG
2016	CLE	RK	18	184	31	10	3	6	27	22	60	10	2	.209/.321/.424
2017	MHV	A-	19	236	29	8	5	10	36	31	80	7	1	.238/.347/.475
2018	LKC	A	20	506	54	11	1	22	58	82	152	12	6	.180/.324/.370
2019	CLE	MLB	21	251	20	4	0	9	25	21	105	1	1	.096/.170/.236

Breakout: 2%   Improve: 5%   Collapse: 1%   Attrition: 3%   MLB: 7%
Comparables: Nomar Mazara, Caleb Gindl, Dylan Cozens

Power remains the calling card for Benson, the toolsy outfielder the Indians plucked with their first-round pick in 2016. In his first look at High-A in his age-20 season, he continued to show the skyscraping ability while questions about his hit tool remain. Benson is already a pretty strict Three True Outcomes guy, even at such a young age, with almost exactly 50 percent of his 2018 plate appearances resulting in either a home run, walk or strikeout. There's a model here for someone who reaches the majors as an above-average contributor, but we're still a few years away figuring out if he can put it all together.

YEAR	TEAM	LVL	AGE	PA	DRC+	VORP	BABIP	BRR	FRAA	WARP
2016	CLE	RK	18	184	89	9.1	.293	2.5	RF(39): -2.0	-0.5
2017	MHV	A-	19	236	107	11.5	.339	0.1	RF(56): -2.5	-0.3
2018	LKC	A	20	506	90	5.6	.218	-0.4	RF(113): 5.4, CF(4): -0.2	0.2
2019	CLE	MLB	21	251	4	-22.4	.109	-0.2	RF 0, CF 0	-2.4

Bobby Bradley 1B

Born: 05/29/96 Age: 23 Bats: L Throws: R
Height: 6'1" Weight: 225 Origin: Round 3, 2014 Draft (#97 overall)

YEAR	TEAM	LVL	AGE	PA	R	2B	3B	HR	RBI	BB	K	SB	CS	AVG/OBP/SLG
2016	LYN	A+	20	572	82	23	1	29	102	75	170	3	0	.235/.344/.466
2017	AKR	AA	21	532	66	25	3	23	89	55	122	3	3	.251/.331/.465
2018	AKR	AA	22	421	49	19	3	24	64	45	105	1	0	.214/.304/.477
2018	COH	AAA	22	128	11	7	2	3	19	11	43	0	0	.254/.323/.430
2019	CLE	MLB	23	173	19	8	1	8	24	13	50	0	0	.204/.267/.420

Breakout: 12% Improve: 29% Collapse: 5% Attrition: 17% MLB: 44%
Comparables: Ryan O'Hearn, Paul Goldschmidt, Jerry Sands

The large adult son made Akron his personal Dinger Town for the second straight season, showing off his one true calling card, power, as nearly 60 percent of his total hits went for extra bases. In an age where one-dimensional sluggers are becoming less and less valuable, Bradley will need to improve either his contact skills or his walk rate — and preferably both — to make the leap from interesting and fun prospect to a legitimately exciting one. That's especially true given that he's a non-factor defensively whose future lies at either first base or designated hitter. The power is real, though, so incremental improvements in any of those areas will likely bring BIG BOY SZN to Cleveland.

YEAR	TEAM	LVL	AGE	PA	DRC+	VORP	BABIP	BRR	FRAA	WARP
2016	LYN	A+	20	572	120	23.4	.293	0.2	1B(116): -6.4	-0.4
2017	AKR	AA	21	532	119	17.6	.287	-2.6	1B(125): -6.3	-0.3
2018	AKR	AA	22	421	107	17.0	.226	-2.3	1B(97): 1.4	0.0
2018	COH	AAA	22	128	99	2.8	.377	0.3	1B(29): 1.5	0.2
2019	CLE	MLB	23	173	77	-1.7	.234	-0.3	1B -1	-0.3

Yu-Cheng Chang SS

Born: 08/18/95 Age: 23 Bats: R Throws: R
Height: 6'1" Weight: 175 Origin: International Free Agent, 2013

YEAR	TEAM	LVL	AGE	PA	R	2B	3B	HR	RBI	BB	K	SB	CS	AVG/OBP/SLG
2016	LYN	A+	20	477	78	30	8	13	70	45	110	11	3	.259/.332/.463
2017	AKR	AA	21	508	72	24	5	24	66	52	134	11	4	.220/.312/.461
2018	COH	AAA	22	518	56	28	2	13	62	44	144	4	3	.256/.330/.411
2019	CLE	MLB	23	202	21	9	1	7	24	13	64	1	1	.212/.274/.386

Breakout: 15% Improve: 26% Collapse: 4% Attrition: 11% MLB: 37%
Comparables: Todd Frazier, Alex Blandino, Trevor Story

Chang's biggest problem in 2018 was something he couldn't do anything about. He was a shortstop/third base prospect playing in the high minors for an organization that happens to have a pair of young 8s holding down those positions in the majors. They aren't going anywhere for awhile. Despite a power dip after moving to Triple-A, Chang possesses solid pull power and isn't afraid to take a walk. His hands should be good enough to stick at shortstop, but at the very least he should be able to handle third base. The question for Chang is whether he'll make enough contact to be a factor once he finally gets there (and whether "there" will be Cleveland).

YEAR	TEAM	LVL	AGE	PA	DRC+	VORP	BABIP	BRR	FRAA	WARP
2016	LYN	A+	20	477	112	35.1	.316	2.9	SS(104): 0.0	1.6
2017	AKR	AA	21	508	102	33.8	.254	2.3	SS(122): 20.3	3.7
2018	COH	AAA	22	518	103	16.6	.341	-3.3	SS(94): -7.3, 3B(23): -0.7	0.3
2019	CLE	MLB	23	202	72	-1.4	.268	-0.2	3B -3, SS 0	-0.4

Tyler Freeman SS
Born: 05/21/99 Age: 20 Bats: R Throws: R
Height: 6'0" Weight: 170 Origin: Round 2, 2017 Draft (#71 overall)

YEAR	TEAM	LVL	AGE	PA	R	2B	3B	HR	RBI	BB	K	SB	CS	AVG/OBP/SLG
2017	CLE	RK	18	144	19	9	0	2	14	7	12	5	1	.297/.364/.414
2018	MHV	A-	19	301	49	29	4	2	38	8	22	14	3	.352/.405/.511
2019	CLE	MLB	20	251	23	9	1	6	20	1	49	2	1	.172/.204/.283

Breakout: 7% Improve: 7% Collapse: 0% Attrition: 1% MLB: 7%
Comparables: Amed Rosario, Ruben Tejada, Wilmer Flores

Freeman's free-swinging approach helped him mash the New York-Penn League as a 19-year-old, living up to what many scouts saw in his hit tool when he was a second-round pick in 2017. He also drew just eight walks in 301 plate appearances, so he'll try to avoid being exposed once he begins facing more advanced competition. He was drafted as a shortstop, though he may get moved to second base before long. Wherever he's standing on the diamond, Freeman's bat will be the difference-maker.

YEAR	TEAM	LVL	AGE	PA	DRC+	VORP	BABIP	BRR	FRAA	WARP
2017	CLE	RK	18	144	121	12.8	.313	1.8	SS(29): -0.1, 2B(4): -0.9	0.3
2018	MHV	A-	19	301	180	37.7	.372	3.5	SS(52): -0.1, 2B(10): -0.2	2.7
2019	CLE	MLB	20	251	30	-11.9	.197	-0.1	SS 0, 2B 0	-1.3

Daniel Johnson RF

Born: 07/11/95 Age: 23 Bats: L Throws: L
Height: 5'10" Weight: 185 Origin: Round 5, 2016 Draft (#154 overall)

YEAR	TEAM	LVL	AGE	PA	R	2B	3B	HR	RBI	BB	K	SB	CS	AVG/OBP/SLG
2016	AUB	A-	20	264	25	9	4	1	14	7	42	13	3	.265/.312/.347
2017	HAG	A	21	364	61	16	4	17	52	22	70	12	9	.300/.361/.529
2017	POT	A+	21	185	22	13	0	5	20	13	30	10	2	.294/.346/.459
2018	HAR	AA	22	391	48	19	7	6	31	23	90	21	4	.267/.321/.410
2019	*CLE*	*MLB*	*23*	*251*	*28*	*7*	*2*	*7*	*23*	*4*	*65*	*6*	*2*	*.203/.228/.339*

Breakout: 5% Improve: 13% Collapse: 0% Attrition: 8% MLB: 13%
Comparables: Mike Gerber, Kyle Waldrop, Andrew Lambo

Were his desired big-league destination still Montreal, this high-variance, tooled-up outfielder might have been the third Daniel Johnson to serve as a Quebec premier … attraction. His first taste of the advanced minors made for a more humble stat line than he's used to, but public Statcast data on his Arizona Fall League exploits raised eyebrows. Said a different way: He traffics in the exit velocity. All of the exit velocity. Shortly after that display, he exited Washington's plans in the Yan Gomes trade, but his power bat and showstopping arm are begging to be seen on a major-league stage.

YEAR	TEAM	LVL	AGE	PA	DRC+	VORP	BABIP	BRR	FRAA	WARP
2016	AUB	A-	20	264	107	8.7	.315	1.6	CF(24): -3.3, RF(24): 1.2	0.1
2017	HAG	A	21	364	140	31.4	.333	-0.5	RF(51): -1.1, CF(15): 0.3	1.7
2017	POT	A+	21	185	118	10.3	.331	1.7	CF(30): -3.2, RF(9): 3.5	0.7
2018	HAR	AA	22	391	95	7.6	.338	-2.3	RF(54): 6.3, CF(33): -2.9	0.2
2019	*CLE*	*MLB*	*23*	*251*	*45*	*-7.7*	*.246*	*1.0*	*RF 0, CF -1*	*-1.0*

Nolan Jones 3B

Born: 05/07/98 Age: 21 Bats: L Throws: R
Height: 6'4" Weight: 185 Origin: Round 2, 2016 Draft (#55 overall)

YEAR	TEAM	LVL	AGE	PA	R	2B	3B	HR	RBI	BB	K	SB	CS	AVG/OBP/SLG
2016	CLE	RK	18	134	10	5	2	0	9	23	49	3	1	.257/.388/.339
2017	MHV	A-	19	265	41	18	3	4	33	43	60	1	0	.317/.430/.482
2018	LKC	A	20	389	46	12	0	16	49	63	97	2	1	.279/.393/.464
2018	LYN	A+	20	130	23	9	0	3	17	26	34	0	0	.298/.438/.471
2019	CLE	MLB	21	251	22	7	0	7	26	26	91	0	0	.164/.251/.291

Breakout: 12% Improve: 19% Collapse: 1% Attrition: 9% MLB: 23%
Comparables: Ryan McMahon, Matt Dominguez, Willy Adames

Jones continued to develop in the exact way Cleveland likely envisioned when they nabbed the prep bat in the second round of the 2016 draft. In his first taste of full-season ball, he eviscerated the Midwest League and more than held his own in a late-season audition at High-A as a 20-year-old, showing patience rivaled by few hitters at the level. A converted shortstop, Jones' defense at the hot corner has been uneven — many believe he'll wind up at first base long term — but he's shown enough athleticism to go along with a plus arm that it's too early to give up on him there yet. If he does stick at third, he could turn into one of the more intriguing prospects in the game.

YEAR	TEAM	LVL	AGE	PA	DRC+	VORP	BABIP	BRR	FRAA	WARP
2016	CLE	RK	18	134	120	7.7	.459	0.2	3B(28): 4.6, SS(5): 0.2	0.7
2017	MHV	A-	19	265	171	28.4	.417	1.7	3B(53): 0.0	2.1
2018	LKC	A	20	389	151	33.5	.347	-0.9	3B(77): -4.1	2.3
2018	LYN	A+	20	130	155	12.7	.418	0.1	3B(28): -0.3	0.9
2019	CLE	MLB	21	251	50	-10.0	.232	-0.6	3B 0	-1.1

Oscar Mercado CF

Born: 12/16/94   Age: 24   Bats: R   Throws: R
Height: 6'2"   Weight: 175   Origin: Round 2, 2013 Draft (#57 overall)

YEAR	TEAM	LVL	AGE	PA	R	2B	3B	HR	RBI	BB	K	SB	CS	AVG/OBP/SLG
2016	PMB	A+	21	506	50	23	1	0	27	44	71	33	20	.215/.296/.271
2017	SFD	AA	22	523	76	20	4	13	46	32	112	38	19	.287/.341/.428
2018	MEM	AAA	23	427	73	21	1	8	42	36	64	31	8	.285/.351/.408
2018	COH	AAA	23	119	12	5	1	0	5	13	23	6	4	.252/.342/.320
2019	CLE	MLB	24	70	8	2	0	2	7	4	17	3	1	.231/.286/.354

Breakout: 14%   Improve: 32%   Collapse: 1%   Attrition: 29%   MLB: 41%
Comparables: Jon Jay, Charlie Blackmon, Gary Brown

The Indians acquired the shortstop-turned-center fielder from the Cardinals in July and added him to the 40-man roster as additional outfield depth in Triple-A. The former second-round pick's specialty is speed, as he can make an impact on the basepaths and has looked the part tracking down fly balls in center. Mercado's bat remains a question and the offensive strides he seemed to make in Memphis weren't as prevalent once he moved to the International League. Mercado is still young enough to hope his hit tool comes around, but even if it doesn't his speed and defense make him an option as a fourth outfielder.

YEAR	TEAM	LVL	AGE	PA	DRC+	VORP	BABIP	BRR	FRAA	WARP
2016	PMB	A+	21	506	81	5.3	.253	1.1	SS(81): 0.9, CF(38): 3.2	0.5
2017	SFD	AA	22	523	113	32.9	.348	5.7	CF(108): -2.1, LF(7): -0.7	1.4
2018	MEM	AAA	23	427	109	32.6	.323	8.1	CF(89): -2.6, LF(7): -0.5	1.8
2018	COH	AAA	23	119	94	-2.3	.325	-2.2	CF(24): -0.8, RF(7): 0.3	-0.1
2019	CLE	MLB	24	70	71	-0.2	.290	0.2	LF 0, RF 0	-0.1

Cleveland Indians 2019

Bo Naylor C
Born: 02/21/00 Age: 19 Bats: L Throws: R
Height: 6'0" Weight: 195 Origin: Round 1, 2018 Draft (#29 overall)

YEAR	TEAM	LVL	AGE	PA	R	2B	3B	HR	RBI	BB	K	SB	CS	AVG/OBP/SLG
2018	CLT	RK	18	139	17	3	3	2	17	21	28	5	1	.274/.381/.402
2019	CLE	MLB	19	251	16	2	1	5	20	17	89	0	0	.123/.180/.202

Breakout: 5% Improve: 7% Collapse: 0% Attrition: 3% MLB: 9%
Comparables: Francisco Pena, Franmil Reyes, Nomar Mazara

Cleveland's 2018 first-round pick has a couple of general factors working against him. Naylor is a prep catcher and was taken at the very end of the first round, both demographics which tend to fare poorly. Still, he held his own in his brief rookie-ball debut and his best tool is probably his ability to make contact. In an era where bat-control hitters make swing-plane adjustments and start uncorking 20-30 home runs, perhaps this profile is worth monitoring more closely. Like his brother, Padres first base prospect Josh Naylor, he's stocky and already quite filled out. He's played some third base, but would likely be destined for first base if he can't stick behind the plate and may not have the power to be very interesting over there.

YEAR	TEAM	LVL	AGE	PA	DRC+	VORP	BABIP	BRR	FRAA	WARP
2018	CLT	RK	18	139	126	12.3	.341	0.3	C(19): -0.4, 3B(5): -0.7	0.3
2019	CLE	MLB	19	251	3	-19.5	.168	0.1	C 0, 3B 0	-2.1

Aaron Civale RHP

Born: 06/12/95   Age: 24   Bats: R   Throws: R
Height: 6'2"   Weight: 215   Origin: Round 3, 2016 Draft (#92 overall)

YEAR	TEAM	LVL	AGE	W	L	SV	G	GS	IP	H	HR	BB/9	K/9	K	GB%	BABIP
2016	MHV	A-	21	0	2	0	13	13	37^2	23	0	1.9	6.7	28	62%	.225
2017	LKC	A	22	2	4	0	10	10	57	64	2	0.8	8.4	53	55%	.358
2017	LYN	A+	22	11	2	0	17	17	107^2	96	11	0.8	7.4	88	49%	.276
2018	AKR	AA	23	5	7	0	21	21	106^1	115	12	1.8	6.6	78	49%	.308
2019	*CLE*	*MLB*	*24*	*5*	*7*	*0*	*19*	*19*	*94^2*	*109*	*16*	*2.7*	*6.5*	*68*	*46%*	*.309*

Breakout: 10%   Improve: 19%   Collapse: 16%   Attrition: 35%   MLB: 41%
Comparables: Ryan Merritt, Richard Bleier, Chad Jenkins

With Shane Bieber reaching the majors and Josh Tomlin on his way out, Cleveland needed a new pitcher to join the Walk Resistance. Enter Civale. The former third-round pick got his first taste of the high minors in 2018 and saw his walk rate increase a bit, but not enough to make the other two furrow their brows in disapproval. Unfortunately for Civale, he's nearly as averse to strikeouts as he is to walks, and until he starts missing more bats it's unclear if he has a future in a big-league rotation.

YEAR	TEAM	LVL	AGE	WHIP	ERA	DRA	WARP	MPH	FB%	WHF	CSP
2016	MHV	A-	21	0.82	1.67	3.16	0.9				
2017	LKC	A	22	1.21	4.58	3.49	1.2				
2017	LYN	A+	22	0.98	2.59	3.55	2.2				
2018	AKR	AA	23	1.28	3.89	3.71	2.0				
2019	*CLE*	*MLB*	*24*	*1.46*	*4.97*	*5.31*	*0.2*				

Cleveland Indians 2019

Ethan Hankins   RHP
Born: 05/23/00   Age: 19   Bats: R   Throws: R
Height: 6'6"   Weight: 200   Origin: Round 1C, 2018 Draft (#35 overall)

YEAR	TEAM	LVL	AGE	W	L	SV	G	GS	IP	H	HR	BB/9	K/9	K	GB%	BABIP
2019	CLE	MLB	19	2	3	0	7	7	31^1	34	5	5.4	8.1	28	40%	.313

Comparables: Bryse Wilson, Jaime Barria, Jamie Callahan

A shoulder injury in his draft year dropped Hankins from a potential top pick to the end of the first round, where Cleveland scooped him up for slightly more than slot to spurn a commitment to Vanderbilt. His fastball can reach the high 90s and has good movement, and he easily blew away hitters with it at the low levels. Believe it or not, as a prep pitcher, he's a volatile prospect with overwhelming upside but high bust potential, but if he lives up to what teams saw out of him before and after his injury, Cleveland will be happy to make the Progressive Field pitcher's mound Hankins' Hill.

YEAR	TEAM	LVL	AGE	WHIP	ERA	DRA	WARP	MPH	FB%	WHF	CSP
2019	CLE	MLB	19	1.68	5.83	6.24	-0.3				

Triston McKenzie RHP

Born: 08/02/97   Age: 21   Bats: R   Throws: R
Height: 6'5"   Weight: 165   Origin: Round 1, 2015 Draft (#42 overall)

YEAR	TEAM	LVL	AGE	W	L	SV	G	GS	IP	H	HR	BB/9	K/9	K	GB%	BABIP
2016	MHV	A-	18	4	3	0	9	9	49^1	31	2	2.9	10.0	55	37%	.248
2016	LKC	A	18	2	2	0	6	6	34	27	2	1.6	13.0	49	40%	.333
2017	LYN	A+	19	12	6	0	25	25	143	105	14	2.8	11.7	186	43%	.283
2018	AKR	AA	20	7	4	0	16	16	90^2	63	8	2.8	8.6	87	34%	.234
2019	CLE	MLB	21	1	1	0	3	3	15	15	3	3.5	8.7	14	35%	.293

Breakout: 6%   Improve: 17%   Collapse: 6%   Attrition: 17%   MLB: 29%
Comparables: Chris Tillman, Jacob Turner, Julio Teheran

Height and weight listings are not permanent, but even if McKenzie isn't quite 6-foot-5 or weighs a few more pounds than 165, it's still safe to characterize him as "lanky." And 2018 gave doubters and believers alike plenty of ammunition. His velocity hasn't ticked up yet, as he continues to sit 88-92 with his fastball, he missed two months with the ever-ominous "forearm soreness" and his strikeout rate dropped significantly in his first look at Double-A. Detractors fear these issues are symptoms of his lack of physicality on the mound, questioning his durability and whether he'll make good on his projectability. Even so, McKenzie may have enough to be a good starting pitcher without a lot more. He uses his height to generate good plane on his pitches with above-average command, and has a genuine out-pitch in his high-70s curve. Even while fighting through injuries, at age 20, he kept his walks down, posted a sub-3.00 ERA against his highest competition yet and, hey, a guy with this build just struck out the side to win the World Series. McKenzie has held serve, failed to dispel the primary doubts about him and yet is now knocking on the door to the majors.

YEAR	TEAM	LVL	AGE	WHIP	ERA	DRA	WARP	MPH	FB%	WHF	CSP
2016	MHV	A-	18	0.95	0.55	2.92	1.3				
2016	LKC	A	18	0.97	3.18	2.33	1.1				
2017	LYN	A+	19	1.05	3.46	2.60	4.5				
2018	AKR	AA	20	1.00	2.68	4.03	1.4				
2019	CLE	MLB	21	1.39	4.69	5.30	0.0				

Cleveland Indians 2019

Danny Salazar   RHP
Born: 01/11/90   Age: 29   Bats: R   Throws: R
Height: 6'0"   Weight: 195   Origin: International Free Agent, 2006

YEAR	TEAM	LVL	AGE	W	L	SV	G	GS	IP	H	HR	BB/9	K/9	K	GB%	BABIP
2016	CLE	MLB	26	11	6	0	25	25	137[1]	121	16	4.1	10.6	161	49%	.307
2017	CLE	MLB	27	5	6	0	23	19	103	94	14	3.8	12.7	145	39%	.343
2019	CLE	MLB	29	5	3	0	28	10	76	65	8	4.0	10.8	92	44%	.300

Breakout: 16%   Improve: 36%   Collapse: 24%   Attrition: 6%   MLB: 86%
Comparables: Lance Lynn, Jonathan Sanchez, Tim Lincecum

It wasn't all that long ago that Salazar was The Next Big Thing as a young right-hander with elite swing-and-miss stuff who seemed close to putting it all together. Bouts of wildness and an inability to stay healthy have kept him from living up to that potential, and he'd been passed in Cleveland's rotation pecking order by Carlos Carrasco and Trevor Bauer even before arthroscopic right shoulder surgery cost him the entirety of 2018. History is littered with guys robbed of what could've been brilliant careers by injuries, and Salazar fits firmly in that category until proven otherwise.

YEAR	TEAM	LVL	AGE	WHIP	ERA	DRA	WARP	MPH	FB%	WHF	CSP
2016	CLE	MLB	26	1.34	3.87	3.79	2.5	97.5	68.3	12	46.1
2017	CLE	MLB	27	1.34	4.28	3.54	2.3	97.2	59.7	17.3	45.8
2019	CLE	MLB	29	1.31	3.29	3.83	1.4	96.7	64	14.7	45.9

LINEOUTS

Hitters

HITTER	POS	TEAM	LVL	AGE	PA	R	2B	3B	HR	RBI	BB	K	SB	CS	AVG/OBP/SLG	DRC+	WARP
Brandon Barnes	OF	COH	AAA	32	566	75	39	2	14	81	47	152	19	5	.273/.347/.444	118	2.8
	OF	CLE	MLB	32	21	2	0	0	1	2	2	5	0	0	.263/.333/.421	93	0.0
Jodd Carter	OF	LYN	A+	21	423	54	20	3	10	52	47	96	11	6	.244/.334/.397	108	0.7
	OF	AKR	AA	21	75	6	0	1	1	4	3	12	0	0	.290/.338/.362	93	-0.3
Gavin Collins	C	LYN	A+	22	252	28	20	1	5	36	14	46	1	2	.232/.293/.395	83	0.1
Raynel Delgado	SS	CLT	Rk	18	204	34	10	0	1	21	30	44	10	2	.306/.409/.382	149	0.9
Tim Federowicz	C	FRE	AAA	30	151	24	13	0	6	22	16	27	0	0	.328/.404/.560	154	1.5
	C	HOU	MLB	30	35	4	3	0	0	2	1	13	0	0	.206/.229/.294	73	0.0
	C	LOU	AAA	30	88	10	6	0	1	9	9	20	0	0	.244/.318/.359	104	0.1
	C	CIN	MLB	30	7	1	1	0	1	2	1	3	0	0	.333/.429/1.000	66	-0.1
Mike Freeman	SS	IOW	AAA	30	331	51	15	2	6	38	25	66	6	6	.274/.330/.396	101	1.4
	SS	CHN	MLB	30	1	0	0	0	0	0	0	0	0	0		91	0.0
Eric Haase	C	COH	AAA	25	477	54	24	3	20	71	31	143	3	1	.236/.288/.443	93	0.0
	C	CLE	MLB	25	17	0	0	0	0	1	0	6	0	0	.125/.176/.125	67	0.0
Logan Ice	C	LYN	A+	23	166	15	5	1	1	21	18	46	0	0	.194/.289/.264	60	-0.5
	C	AKR	AA	23	55	8	3	2	0	8	5	18	0	0	.250/.315/.396	68	-0.1
Max Moroff	SS	PIT	MLB	25	67	7	1	0	3	9	7	24	0	0	.186/.284/.356	73	-0.1
	SS	IND	AAA	25	297	38	14	2	8	38	43	68	5	0	.223/.334/.393	111	0.7
Mike Papi	OF	COH	AAA	25	296	38	17	1	7	26	47	78	1	1	.247/.373/.412	120	1.3
Brayan Rocchio	INF	DIN	Rk	17	111	19	2	3	1	12	5	14	8	5	.323/.391/.434	137	0.6
	INF	CLT	Rk	17	158	21	10	1	1	17	10	17	14	8	.343/.389/.448	166	1.5
Eric Stamets	INF	COH	AAA	26	269	22	10	2	5	16	18	63	5	2	.202/.272/.324	54	0.1

In 2013, **Brandon Barnes** was the starting center fielder for a Houston Astros team that went 51-111. In 2018, he was the guy you'd see when you took your family to a Columbus Clippers game and think "there's no way he's *that* Brandon Barnes." ⓧ A relatively undersized 24th-round pick whose parents named him "Jodd," he's plugged away in the low minors for five years and began scraping up against Double-A. Still, **Jodd Carter** of Mars has yet to demonstrate any specific carrying tool and he's likely org depth. ⓧ Evidently the Indians just love splitting their prospects between catching and third base. Unfortunately, 2018 represented a step backwards at the plate when **Gavin Collins** wasn't on the shelf with a back injury. ⓧ The Indians took the Cuban-born **Raynel Delgado** in the sixth round and gave him second-round money to bypass a commitment to Florida International. Early reports show an above-average command of the strike zone and a chance to stick at shortstop. ⓧ **Tim Federowicz**, the perennial backup to the backup catcher, finds another team and nets another 15 games for his MLB career scrapbook. That's it. That's the whole story. ⓧ Minor-league journeyman **Mike Freeman** is probably getting jittery from all the cups of coffee he's had. His latest, clocking in at exactly one plate appearance, certainly did not satisfy his cravings. ⓧ **Erik Haase** flashed good power at Triple-A, proving the spike that earned him a 40-man roster spot in 2017 was no fluke. His lack of receiving skills might make it difficult for this Haase to find a long-term home in the majors. ⓧ Not to be confused with a limited release beer used to promote a Wolverine movie or the finance bro who always managed to smuggle Smirnoff into your desk, **Logan Ice** is a former college catcher who's yet to hit after three years the low minors. ⓧ A versatile fielder with a good batting eye, **Max Moroff** once again looked over-matched against big-league pitching, particularly against the hard stuff. ⓧ The former first-round pick and bat-first prospect forgot to bring his big stick with him in his second go at Triple-A. **Mike Papi**'s walk rate remains the calling card, but his power was virtually non-existent and he saw a significant uptick in strikeouts. ⓧ It may be passe to use batting average or prospect stat lines, but when a 17-year-old middle infielder hits .335 with decent walks and power it's worth taking notice. **Brayan Rocchio** may be an actual shortstop and has pretty good speed paired with potentially strong contact skills. ⓧ **Nellie Rodriguez** has spent two years mashing Double-A while failing to do the same at Triple-A. As a first base-only prospect nearing his mid-20s, it's unclear if any organization will be willing to take a ride with him. ⓧ The glove-first prospect isn't really a prospect any more, as **Eric Stamets** is older than the two MVP candidates on the left side of Cleveland's infield and his OPS in Triple-A started with the number 5. ⓧ **George Valera** signed for $1.3 million as an international free agent despite being born in New York and made his pro debut in 2018. It wound up being brief, as he broke a hamate bone, but the stats are pretty and there's a lot to like here in terms of projectable raw power.

Pitchers

PITCHER	TEAM	LVL	AGE	W	L	SV	G	GS	IP	H	HR	BB/9	K/9	K	GB%	WHIP	ERA	DRA	WARP
Adam Cimber	SDN	MLB	27	3	5	0	42	0	48^1	42	2	1.9	9.5	51	53%	1.08	3.17	3.92	0.6
	CLE	MLB	27	0	3	0	28	0	20	26	3	3.2	3.2	7	68%	1.65	4.05	6.17	-0.3
Jon Edwards	AKR	AA	30	0	1	0	9	0	9^2	6	1	5.6	13.0	14	45%	1.24	3.72	1.84	0.3
	COH	AAA	30	2	1	4	25	0	30	23	2	2.7	12.6	42	37%	1.07	3.60	2.75	0.8
	CLE	MLB	30	0	0	0	9	0	8^2	6	2	4.2	10.4	10	48%	1.15	3.12	2.51	0.2
Nick Goody	CLE	MLB	26	0	2	0	12	0	11^2	15	4	3.9	9.3	12	30%	1.71	6.94	5.33	-0.1
Justin Grimm	KCA	MLB	29	1	3	0	16	0	12^2	17	2	9.9	5.7	8	44%	2.45	13.50	7.86	-0.4
	SEA	MLB	29	0	0	0	5	0	4^2	2	1	0.0	5.8	3	23%	0.43	1.93	3.50	0.1
Sam Hentges	LYN	A+	21	6	6	0	23	23	118^1	114	4	4.0	9.3	122	41%	1.41	3.27	3.99	1.9
Juan Hillman	LKC	A	21	6	12	0	26	26	128^2	140	7	3.6	7.7	110	46%	1.49	5.18	5.10	0.2
James Hoyt	HOU	MLB	31	0	0	0	1	0	0^1	1	0	27.0	0.0	0	100%	6.00	0.00	2.07	0.0
	FRE	AAA	31	0	3	5	25	0	28	19	2	2.6	10.6	33	52%	0.96	2.25	2.68	0.8
Luis Oviedo	MHV	A-	19	4	2	0	9	9	48	34	3	1.9	11.4	61	52%	0.92	1.88	3.31	1.1
	LKC	A	19	1	0	0	2	2	9	5	0	7.0	6.0	6	44%	1.33	3.00	4.44	0.1
Adam Plutko	COH	AAA	26	7	3	0	14	14	84^2	47	5	1.7	8.6	81	29%	0.74	1.70	3.88	1.6
	CLE	MLB	26	4	5	1	17	12	76^2	78	21	2.7	7.0	60	29%	1.32	5.28	7.22	-1.7
Jefry Rodriguez	HAR	AA	24	5	3	0	13	13	68	55	6	3.7	9.5	72	53%	1.22	3.31	3.37	1.6
	SYR	AAA	24	2	2	0	6	6	32^2	32	0	4.1	8.3	30	47%	1.44	3.58	4.45	0.4
	WAS	MLB	24	3	3	0	14	8	52	43	8	6.4	6.8	39	46%	1.54	5.71	7.35	-1.3
Nick Sandlin	LKC	A	21	0	0	1	10	0	10^1	9	0	0.0	13.1	15	52%	0.87	1.74	1.08	0.5
	LYN	A+	21	1	0	4	7	0	6^1	2	0	2.8	14.2	10	50%	0.63	1.42	2.43	0.2
Ben Taylor	CLE	MLB	25	0	0	0	6	0	6	6	2	1.5	12.0	8	50%	1.17	6.00	4.80	0.0
	COH	AAA	25	7	2	11	46	0	57^1	42	5	1.4	11.0	70	42%	0.89	2.51	3.07	1.3
Lenny Torres	CLT	Rk	17	0	0	0	6	5	15^1	14	0	2.3	12.9	22	51%	1.17	1.76	2.98	0.5
Nick Wittgren	NWO	AAA	27	0	5	2	25	0	29^1	34	4	2.5	10.4	34	46%	1.43	5.22	2.94	0.7
	MIA	MLB	27	2	1	0	32	0	33^2	29	1	4.0	8.3	31	46%	1.31	2.94	3.81	0.4

Brady Aiken went no. 1 overall in the 2014 draft and has been relegated to Lineout status five years later, which says more about how his career has gone than anything. ⓦ Cleveland's lesser Cody A. had a brutal sophomore year in 2016 before missing all of 2017 and all but three innings of 2018 recovering from Tommy John surgery. We should see **Cody Anderson** back in 2019. After all, tell me, Mr. Anderson, what good is positive regression if you're unable to pitch? ⓦ When asked to describe the right-handed submariner's arm action, Ke$ha said, "It's going down, I'm yelling Cimber." She declined to comment on **Adam**

Cleveland Indians 2019

Cimber's peripherals. ⓧ **Oliver Drake** looked like a good fit for the Indians, at least until he ran into the Astros. Thirty minutes and two-thirds of an inning later, his ERA was three runs higher and he was heading off to his third team of the season. ⓧ O pitcher! Consider the fearful danger you are in. You hang by a slender thread, with the flames of awful command flashing about it, and ready every moment to singe it, and burn it asunder. (Jonathan Edwards. **Jon Edwards**. Whatever.) ⓧ After breaking through as a solid middle reliever in 2017, **Nick Goody** suffered an elbow injury early in 2018 and missed the remainder of the season, which is bad-y. ⓧ For years **Justin Grimm** built his success in large part on his ability to get hitters to chase pitches out of the strike zone. His stuff has degraded to the point where that they don't do that much anymore, and now his name serves as a very full and complete self-scouting report. ⓧ A fourth-round pick in 2014, **Sam Hentges** has been brought along slowly by Cleveland since undergoing Tommy John surgery, but put himself back on the radar with a strong showing in High-A. His fastball sits mid-90s and he his off-speed stuff shows enough potential to stick as a mid-rotation arm. ⓧ **Juan Hillman** repeated the Midwest League and showed the same command issues that plagued him a year earlier. His age and the fact that he has three potential above-average offerings still make the former second-round pick someone to wait on. ⓧ Spamming sliders is the new hotness, which is good news because that's basically all **James Hoyt** can do. Hoyt lost most of 2018 buried on the Astros' relief depth chart and on the disabled list, but there's a major-league reliever here. ⓧ It's been five years since **Alexi Ogando** was anything resembling an effective major-league reliever, but he threw one inning in the majors in May for some reason so he qualifies for the book. ⓧ The projection Cleveland saw in **Luis Oviedo** when they signed him for $375,000 out of Venezuela in 2015 started to pay dividends in 2018, as he passed his first test at a level above complex ball, showing good velocity with his fastball to go along with three developing breaking pitches. ⓧ **Adam Plutko** spent most of 2018 riding back and forth on the Columbus-to-Cleveland shuttle, with the highlight being a Triple-A no-hitter on June 2. ⓧ Last seen returning from a PED suspension, 25-year-old **Jefry Rodriguez** hit the bigs after 13 good Double-A starts and turned every batter he faced into a plate discipline savant, walking 37 and striking out 39. ⓧ **Nick Sandlin** zoomed through the low minors before a late-season call-up to Double-A. With a mid-90s fastball and developing slider, he could see the majors as soon as 2019. ⓧ A team that shuffled through mediocre relievers like a family's White Elephant gift exchange couldn't find a spot for **Ben Taylor** outside of six random May appearances. With a generic name to go along with his generic stuff, he's about as anonymous a reliever as one can find. ⓧ The Indians took **Lenny Torres** no. 41 in the 2018 draft and handed him $1.35 million to bypass St. John's. He dominated at the prep level with a fastball that sat mid-90s, and will need to develop his slider and changeup to have a future in the rotation. ⓧ **Nick Wittgren**'s three-pitch mix is good enough to let him carve a niche in the back end of a bullpen, but not good enough to let the world know he exists.

Indians Prospects

The State of the System:
Cleveland's system is bolstered by a strong 2018 draft class and a couple IFA breakouts in the low minors, but that also means limited help for the big club in the near term.

The Top Ten:

1. Triston McKenzie RHP
OFP: 60   Likely: 55   ETA: Late 2019/Early 2020
Born: 08/02/97   Age: 21   Bats: R   Throws: R   Height: 6'5"   Weight: 165
Origin: Round 1, 2015 Draft (#42 overall)

The Report: This would all be easier if McKenzie were left-handed. It would fit more neatly. It feels like he should be left-handed. Yes, he's still rail-thin so we can all still call him projectable, but the fastball is also still pinned around 90, albeit with good plane and plus command. It's an above-average pitch regardless of stalker readings. There's the same plus mid-70s curve that McKenzie might command even better than the fastball. That's the start of a very nice pitching prospect, but one that is usually a southpaw. I have no idea if that should matter, or if this weirdness is located merely in my head. He throws his changeup sparingly and doesn't have ideal velocity separation, but it's potentially average as well. McKenzie is in Double-A now. He's knocking on the door of the majors. The stuff is fine, better than fine really. He's never had issues getting minor-league hitters out, and the whole profile still feels like a Top 50 prospect. Yet the cognitive dissonance remains.

Oh yeah, McKenzie also missed the first few months with a "forearm," as Al Michaels would say. That's a little more concrete, but maybe not meaningful. We'll see.

The Risks: Medium. He's always been good on the mound, and has been on the mound more often than not. He pitched well in Double-A at 20. Still, McKenzie is rail-thin and missed time this year with an arm injury. We can't write "low."

Bret Sayre's Fantasy Take: McKenzie remains the top fantasy prospect in this system, but it's almost by default and he's getting close to relinquishing that honor. The lack of a high-end ceiling hurts, but his combination of ETA and command helps solidify an SP4 future that could be coming as soon as later this year.

Cleveland Indians 2019

2 | **Luis Oviedo   RHP** | OFP: 60   Likely: 50   ETA: 2021
Born: 05/15/99   Age: 20   Bats: R   Throws: R   Height: 6'4"   Weight: 170
Origin: International Free Agent, 2015

The Report: Ah, the fun of signing 16-year-old Dominican arms. Oviedo was a projectable righty sitting in the upper-80s when he signed. He's now got an ideal starting pitcher's frame and often sits in the mid-90s. The fastball can run a little true at times, but there's enough armside wiggle to keep it off barrels and he commands it well gloveside at present—although the control is still ahead of the command generally. His mechanics are fairly clean, and while there is a bit of late torque and twist, I don't see it meaningfully inhibiting his long-term command projection.

Oviedo added a slider in 2017 and this year it looked like a potential monster out-pitch down the line. At its best it had big, late two-plane break that he could locate to the back foot of lefties. His curve offers a different look, although it's a bit on the loopy side when he tries to spot it in the zone, and at others it can be slurvy and bleed into the slider. Still, there's enough feel to project it to average at maturity. The same is true of the change, which is inconsistent and often firm, but flashes good sink.

Despite the control/command blip in Lake County, there really isn't much to dislike with Oviedo's profile. He's a long way from the majors and mostly physically maxed, but the stuff is really good and doesn't require much refinement. He's probably the youngest arm we will throw into our mid-rotation starter or late-inning reliever bucket on the back of the 101, but that undersells both his upside and realistic floor a little.

The Risks: High. There's only a short-season track record here, and he is a pitcher after all. Sometimes pop-up velocity guys give some of it back as they get stretched out in the pros more.

Bret Sayre's Fantasy Take: Can I interest you in trading nearly all of that certainty for a bit of ceiling? Why, of course. Oviedo has the potential to miss a lot of bats, but we've said that about countless other arms with little to no full-season experience. There are enough ways this can break to fill a Choose Your Own Adventure novel, but the 1-in-5 chance that he breaks right and turns into a future SP2 is very alluring if you prefer to deal in quantity when it comes to fantasy pitching prospects.

3 | **George Valera   OF** | OFP: 60   Likely: 45   ETA: 2023
Born: 11/13/00   Age: 18   Bats: L   Throws: L   Height: 5'10"   Weight: 160
Origin: International Free Agent, 2017

The Report: Valera was one of the top prospects available in the 2017 IFA class. He got paid accordingly. He got brought stateside immediately, which is a slightly aggressive baseball assignment, if less so an acculturation one as he was born in Queens and spent most of his childhood in New York. He played a grand total of six official pro games before being shut down with a hamate injury. Those are the background deets. Primarily what we are betting on here is a very pretty left-handed swing with plus bat speed. God knows there are far worse things to bet on in, well, life really, but it's going to have to the lion's share of carrying the profile. Valera will likely get reps in all three outfield spots for a while, but he's already filling out so I'll just mention he has the arm for right. He might not have the power for either corner, but we won't know any of this for sure for a half decade, so just roll that beautiful swing footage for now.

The Risks: Extreme. He's a teenager who might not stick up-the-middle, has played exactly six professional games, and will be coming off a hamate injury.

Bret Sayre's Fantasy Take: For my money, short of Wander Franco, there's not a better fantasy prospect who hasn't reached full-season ball than Valera. The swing portends a .300-plus, 25-homer future and while he's a very long way off, I will fight Ben to claw him up as high on the 101 as I can.

4

Nolan Jones 3B   OFP: 55   Likely: 45   ETA: Late 2020/Early 2021
Born: 05/07/98   Age: 21   Bats: L   Throws: R   Height: 6'4"   Weight: 185
Origin: Round 2, 2016 Draft (#55 overall)

The Report: Jones is a prospect who would fit quite neatly into our old Good/Bad format, so let's give it a spin:

The Good: Jones converted some of his ample raw power into games and did so as a 20-year-old in a difficult hitting environment. The swing has always been geared for plus pull-side power, while he tended to work more gap-to-gap, but Jones managed to marry the two without adding substantial swing-and-miss. He's unlikely to get all of his plus raw into games, as the swing can get long when he goes for it, but both offensive tools look more likely to reach solid-average than they did last year.

The Bad: It's still unclear where Jones' long term defensive home is. Errors are a bad way to measure minor-league defense, but his range and hands don't pass muster yet either. Jones has filled out enough—he looks about 20 pounds or so heavier than the weight above—where a move to left field or first base might be on the offer eventually, putting an awful lot of pressure on his bat.

The Risks: Medium. The bat has taken a big step forward and his performance in A-ball matched it, but there's still significant role/positional risk in the profile.

Bret Sayre's Fantasy Take: The step forward in power is certainly encouraging, but it still doesn't raise his ceiling to a potential top-10 option at the position. The average isn't likely to be a positive contribution, though the approach could lead his on-base percentage to be one, and without big-time power, the entire profile just falls a bit short. He'd certainly make a top-150 at this point, but I don't think he belongs among the top 101.

Cleveland Indians 2019

5 **Sam Hentges LHP** OFP: 55 Likely: 45 ETA: Early 2020
Born: 07/18/96 Age: 22 Bats: L Throws: L Height: 6'6" Weight: 245
Origin: Round 4, 2014 Draft (#128 overall)

The Report: I may have gotten a bit of feedback from inside baseball for leaving Hentges off our Cleveland list last year. Fair play, they were likely right. Now, he was a fourth-round prep arm coming off Tommy John surgery who had pitched to a 6 ERA in A-ball before going under the knife, but that's a minor quibble, no?

There's no quibbling with Hentges' 2018 season. The big lefty got back on the mound and showed a potential plus fastball/curve combination. The heater routinely touched 95 with armside run, and Hentges commands it well to both sides of the plate. His high-70s curve shows above-average 12-6 break, while the changeup is projectable, but presently below-average. Hentges is still building up arm strength coming off TJ, but is otherwise in the general range of "interesting mid-rotation arm with third pitch concerns." A lefty with a MLB-quality fastball/curve combo always has a relief fall back, but given the frame and relatively clean delivery, Hentges is a solid bet to stick in a rotation, health and continued refinement permitting.

The Risks: Medium. There's a fair bit of polish here, but Hentges has a recent Tommy John on his resume and has yet to pitch in Double-A.

Bret Sayre's Fantasy Take: The road to fantasy purgatory was laid with mid-rotation pitching prospects, yet we still keep pressing on. Mostly because one out of every 10 of these guys turns into Patrick Corbin or Mike Clevinger rather than Franklin Morales or Deolis Guerra. That said, Hentges is one of the better ones to grab in leagues that roster 200 or more prospects given that his cost is likely to be minimal and you won't have to wait much longer than this calendar year to figure out if you should toss him back in order to gamble on a different future SP4.

6 **Yu-Cheng Chang IF** OFP: 55 Likely: 45
ETA: 2019, when someone gets hurt
Born: 08/18/95 Age: 23 Bats: R Throws: R Height: 6'1" Weight: 175
Origin: International Free Agent, 2013

The Report: Last year's Cleveland list was peppered from top to bottom with three-true-outcome bats, but only Chang really maintained his value proposition in 2018. It helps that he's a passable, if fringy, shortstop. His International League performance was solid, and his scouting report looks similar a year later. The profile remaining more or less the same at a higher level is always good on balance; it's just not the most exciting profile in the world. Chang is probably going to slide over to third in the majors—which won't exactly open additional playing time in Cleveland either—and while he has the raw power for the hot corner, a fringe-average hit tool means it's likely to play down to average in games. Hitting .250 with some pop and the ability to play three infield positions is useful—though again, less so in Cleveland—just not exciting.

The Risks: Medium. There's some risk the hit tool doesn't play at the highest level, more significant risk he has to move off shortstop.

Bret Sayre's Fantasy Take: You're basically closing your eyes and hoping that Chang turns into Aledmys Diaz, and no one wants Aledmys Diaz. Just the mere mention of Aledmys Diaz caused you to move on to the next player on this list. The more open and honest we are about this, the healthier it is for us all.

7 Ethan Hankins   RHP   OFP: 55   Likely: 45   ETA: 2023
Born: 05/23/00   Age: 19   Bats: R   Throws: R   Height: 6'6"   Weight: 200
Origin: Round 1C, 2018 Draft (#35 overall)

The Report: Every year, usually around this time in fact, draftniks start talking themselves into another "Great Right Hope." Yes, this will be the year a prep righty finally goes 1.1. It never happens for a variety of reasons, sometimes injury, other times just remembering that prep righties tend to be among the worst investments you can make in the first round. Hankins was the 2018 Great Right Hope, but a shoulder injury early in the season scuttled any slim chance he had of going first overall.

When he's fully healthy, Hankins offers present mid-90s heat with movement and plenty of projection left as well. He has a remarkably advanced changeup for a prep pitcher, and the curveball will flash. Sure, it wasn't exactly Casey Mize even before the arm issues, but when healthy, Hankins might have more upside than last year's 1:1. There's a chance that the roles below will look hopelessly out of date by the end of April; on the other hand, I did use the phrase "shoulder injury" in this report.

The Risks: High. He's a prep righty who needs a more consistent breaking ball and whose senior season was marred by a shoulder injury. You could certainly argue for "extreme" here if you like.

Bret Sayre's Fantasy Take: If you're going to bet on a prep arm out of the draft, might as well go with one who scraped triple digits before falling into injury purgatory. He's a fine flier in the third round or later, depending on how large your league is, in dynasty formats this winter as he's unlikely to go with a top-30 pick and still carries a fair amount of strikeout upside.

8 Lenny Torres   RHP   OFP: 55   Likely: 45   ETA: 2023
Born: 10/15/00   Age: 18   Bats: R   Throws: R   Height: 6'1"   Weight: 190
Origin: Round 1, 2018 Draft (#41 overall)

The Report: I don't have particularly strong feelings about the order of Cleveland's top three 2018 picks—you can toss in Rocchio too—but if this was closer to a personal pref list, I would have Torres ahead. There's not a real objective reason I can point to, mind you—that's why they call it a pref list.

Hankins looks the part of a high-pick prep starter. He's 6'6", has a projectable frame, and a potential four-pitch mix with two-to-three above-average offerings down the road.

Torres is on the shorter side—although having just turned 18, he might add an inch or two still—and a cold-weather prep arm. The delivery is uptempo, the arm action has some effort. He's primarily fastball/slider, albeit with a potential plus slider and a fastball that popped even more post-draft. The changeup is of course mostly theoretical. Torres is a plus athlete, and I suppose notably, hasn't had a bout of shoulder soreness. Well, not yet anyway; he is a pitcher after all. The reliever risk here is not insubstantial, but what good pitching prospect doesn't carry that burden nowadays?

The Risks: High. Take the Hankins risks, subtract the shoulder woes, add in cold-weather prep arm and less developed secondaries.

Bret Sayre's Fantasy Take: While it's never a bad idea to gamble on the high-velocity guy, it's also never a bad idea to gamble on the "obnoxiously young for his draft class" guy. Torres was the youngest player of note drafted last June and while that's a more meaningful fun fact with hitters than pitchers, it's still notable. I'd take Hankins before Torres in a dynasty draft, but at that point, everyone looks both good and bad simultaneously.

9. Bo Naylor C
OFP: 55   Likely: 45   ETA: 2023
Born: 02/21/00   Age: 19   Bats: L   Throws: R   Height: 6'0"   Weight: 195
Origin: Round 1, 2018 Draft (#29 overall)

The Report: Rumored at various times to be in play for an underslot deal early in the first round, Naylor wound up signing for slightly overslot with Cleveland at the 29th pick. We've long waxed on these web pages about the risks inherent in drafting high school catchers, and Naylor's lower half might remind you a bit too much of his older brother Josh's at that age. Derriere isn't destiny though, and while Naylor is a project behind the plate he has sneaky athleticism for his size and a strong throwing arm. Cleveland got him some reps at third as well, and he could be more of a modern "positionless baseball" backstop where he spends a couple days a week in the field to ease the strain on his body and get his bat into the lineup.

It's a nice bat too. Naylor has plus bat speed with good whip and enough leverage to show off some game power without striking out too often. He is still a cold weather prep bat of course, so there's risk on both the offensive and defensive sides—and a long horizon to major-league utility—but Naylor may end up a very modern draft and development story. Also a very old one: sometimes you just take the guy you think will hit.

The Risks: High. It's the usual prep catcher risks, plus he's less likely to be a long-term every day catcher.

Bret Sayre's Fantasy Take: Of course, I'd take Naylor over both of those pitchers. Short of Valera, Naylor has the best hit tool in this system and while being a catcher should technically disqualify him as an interesting fantasy prospect, there's enough offensive potential and athleticism for him to move off the position. It's a risky profile, for sure, but a .290 average and 20-25 bombs is valuable whether he's still squatting in three years or not.

10

Brayan Rocchio   SS   OFP: 55   Likely: 45   ETA: 2024
Born: 01/13/01   Age: 18   Bats: B   Throws: R   Height: 5'10"   Weight: 150
Origin: International Free Agent, 2017

The Report: Rocchio has quickly turned into a low-six-figure coup for Cleveland. There's a lot to work with here as far as "shortstop prospects born two months after *Mass Romantic* was released" go. He's a switch hitter with good feel for contact from both sides. He's an above-average runner with a good shot to stick at shortstop. The frame could go in a variety of different ways across the rest of his teenage years and into his early 20s, but the swing is contact over power at present, and Rocchio doesn't have a ton of present physicality. He just turned 18, so the delta in the profile is huge, but he's definitely worth watching.

The Risks: Extreme. I'm writing a 2024 ETA below. I will be 42. I'll be in relaxed fit Dad jeans before he's in the majors. Anyway, he's a complex league shortstop who didn't get a huge bonus.

Bret Sayre's Fantasy Take: It's never easy to tell just how high a fantasy ceiling is when a player hasn't taken a single at-bat as an adult, but the plate discipline junkies will get excited that he barely struck out as a 17-year-old spanning complex leagues in two different countries. Take a flier, why not. Otherwise just shrug and see how 2019 goes. He should be rostered in leagues where 250 prospects are owned just in case he makes the jump.

The Next Five:

11

Nick Sandlin   RHP
Born: 01/10/97   Age: 22   Bats: R   Throws: R   Height: 5'11"   Weight: 175
Origin: Round 2, 2018 Draft (#67 overall)

Sandlin was arguably the most dominant starting pitcher in college this year, posting a 1.06 ERA and striking out nearly 13 per nine for Southern Mississippi. This wouldn't be notable past being, well, notable, except for the fact that Sandlin is (mostly) a sidearmer. He will move his slot around, but mostly everything is coming in low. Cleveland drafted him as a quick-moving pen arm—he was a reliever his first two years of college—and he hasn't disappointed so far. He has more fastball than your typical low-armslot guy, sitting in the low-90s and touching higher. Sandlin leans heavily on his slider, which is already plus, and he uses a slower curve as a change of pace as well. He has advanced control and command of the whole arsenal and could very well be the first 2018 draftee to reach the big leagues.

12 James Karinchak   RHP
Born: 09/22/95   Age: 23   Bats: R   Throws: R   Height: 6'3"   Weight: 230
Origin: Round 9, 2017 Draft (#282 overall)

Karinchak doesn't have the same amateur pedigree as Sandlin—he was a ninth-round pick out of Bryant in 2017—but he has similar upside in the pen. The fastball is borderline elite, sitting 95-97 with deception from his funky mechanics and plane from his high slot. There's enough wiggle to keep it off barrels, and it's a swing-and-miss offering on its own. He pairs it with a plus 12-6 curve that comes out of the hand just like the heater. Karinchak dominated three levels in his first professional season, and it's no-doubt closer stuff when he's in or even around the zone. But the combination of the mechanics and effort in the delivery has led to well-below-average control so far. Iron that out, and Cleveland may have found their next reliever monster.

13 Bobby Bradley   1B
Born: 05/29/96   Age: 23   Bats: L   Throws: R   Height: 6'1"   Weight: 225
Origin: Round 3, 2014 Draft (#97 overall)

I'm not entirely sure why Cleveland had Bradley repeat Double-A, but he more or less matched his 2017 performance minus 30 points of batting average and plus a few extra bombs. His brief stint in Triple-A was more bust than boom, however. He's still only 22 and projects as the same three-true-outcome slugger he did last year, but Adam Dunn and Joey Gallo—heck, even Jack Cust—beat up the minors a lot more than Bradley did, so you wonder how the swing is gonna fare against the best arms in the sport. But even in our launch-a-ball era, 30 dingers plays, and Bradley has at least that much power in his locker.

14 Will Benson   OF
Born: 06/16/98   Age: 21   Bats: L   Throws: L   Height: 6'5"   Weight: 225
Origin: Round 1, 2016 Draft (#14 overall)

If you want to get a gauge on what 80 grade raw power looks like, watch Benson take batting practice sometime. It's light-tower power and the ball jumps off the bat making that sound. It's generated by his massive strength and a swing that features natural loft. However, since being drafted 14th overall in 2016, Benson hasn't shown the ability to hit any type of secondary pitches. Low-A pitchers feasted when they got ahead in the count, enticing Benson to chase breaking stuff in and out of the zone. Defensively he's an asset, profiling as an above average right fielder with a cannon for an arm. There's star potential here, with elite power and strong defensive tools, but his issues at the plate make that outcome pretty unlikely.

15 Eric Haase C
Born: 12/18/92   Age: 26   Bats: R   Throws: R   Height: 5'10"   Weight: 180
Origin: Round 7, 2011 Draft (#218 overall)

After a breakout in 2017 while repeating Double-A, Haase fell back to earth some in Columbus last year. We had concerns about the hit tool even when he was mashing in the Eastern League, and Haase struck out 30% of the time in 2018. The swing is stiff and leveraged to get to his plus raw power, and while Haase still got to enough of it to make him a viable backup catcher, you'd like the glove to be a bit better than it is. He has a strong throwing arm, but his receiving is still rough, and Cleveland brought in Kevin Plawecki to pair with Roberto Perez. That leaves Haase on the outside looking in until his defense improves. But you always need catchers: Plawecki's health track record isn't great and Perez is a career .205 hitter. Haase may get another shot with the big club before long.

Top Talents 25 and Under (born 4/1/93 or later):

1. Francisco Lindor
2. Triston McKenzie
3. Shane Bieber
4. Luis Oviedo
5. Jake Bauers
6. George Valera
7. Nolan Jones
8. Sam Hentges
9. Yu-Cheng Chang
10. Ethan Hankins

Since he debuted on June 14, 2015—which could've been a holiday in Cleveland if not for the Cavaliers losing Game 5 of the NBA Finals that night—Francisco Lindor has taken more plate appearances than any other major-leaguer. This is, of course, to the great joy of Cleveland and baseball fans alike. He's reached base in 35 percent of those 2,590 trips to the plate, and sparked dozens of GIFs with his vibrant smile along the way.

A 2017 swing change unlocked more power, but also an adjustment period where Lindor's OBP temporarily sank while he became perhaps a bit too enamored with fly ball contact. In 2018 it popped right back up: the power improvements stuck, and now you can confidently pencil in 6-WARP as a baseline for Lindor. He might be the betting favorite for third-best player in the game, even if that's in a thin-stretched plurality.

Beyond Mr. Smile and just-graduated star Jose Ramirez, the Indians' ranks of bankable young talent are thin enough to give you a long face. Bradley Zimmer aged off this list without proving his bat can support even elite center-field defense. Francisco Mejia was shipped off for relievers and replaced by catching jetsam. Much of the star-level promise on this list has yet to experience the thrills and spills of High-A.

The young player who emerged as a contributor in Cleveland last year was instead Shane Bieber. His first 114 2/3 innings adequately introduced the schtick: Dude doesn't walk anyone. Got it. But this isn't New Josh Tomlin. His 4.7 percent walk rate ranked only 14th among major leaguers who threw 100 innings; Nathan Eovaldi and Joe Musgrove gave out fewer free passes. The bigger surprise is that they also had lower strikeout rates than Bieber. Can that FIP-tastic combo continue apace? Well… he's living on a ton of called strikes and a 93-mph fastball without much bat-missing potential. In a year or two, he may get us to believe in his Old Zack Greinke skillset, but for now, there's still concern that he'll get walloped.

Picked up from the Rays for Yandy Diaz, Jake Bauers apparently showed enough as a rookie to be traded instead of DFA'd. That's a joke, but despite some prospect pedigree and a present-day position in Cleveland, his first 388 major league plate appearances cut the shape of a replaceable hitter and raised serious questions. See, Bauers—whose high walk and low strikeout rates impressed in the upper minors—swung at only 40 percent of the pitches he saw in the majors. It's an extremely low number in general, but perhaps a harmfully passive one for someone with a low contact rate. Of the 30 big-league hitters (min. 300 PA) who offered less frequently than Bauers, only two (Max Muncy and Jose Bautista) missed as often. That's how he ended up striking out 26.8 percent of the time after barely exceeding the 20 percent mark in Triple-A. Combine it with a propensity to feed the shift, and you wind up with a confounding .201/.316/.384 line.

So, did expectations ride on the back of a smart approach? Or on the control issues of the young and the mediocre? Even while piling up those intriguing BB:K ratios, he didn't really drive the ball. His slugging percentage over a full year at Double-A was .420. In Bauers' full Triple-A season, 2017, he slugged .412. Those numbers are fine, but among fast-tracked prospects they were more akin to middle infielders like then-teammate Willy Adames and J.P. Crawford than corner-occupying mashers. It's reasonable to expect base-reaching patience to come with power-boosting pitch selection, but Bauers really needs to show evidence of the latter to make it at first or in left—and that's not even mentioning his platoon issue.

Jordan Luplow didn't make the list, but he's the next most likely 25-year-old to make an impact in Cleveland this year. The corner outfielder, acquired from Pittsburgh, would sound a bit like Bauers if he were left-handed—good approach, strong numbers in the upper minors, power potential. But as it is, he'll be fighting to escape the short side of a platoon and prove that the pop is worth a boatload of fly balls. They have mostly fallen into gloves in the majors thus far, torpedoing his production. Still, he avoids strikeouts well and may have a crazy 2017 Yonder Alonso season in him somewhere.

Part 3: Featured Articles

The Hole in The Shift is Fixing Itself

Russell Carleton

I've been on a bit of a mission against The Shift of late. I'm not out to get The Shift for the usual reasons that people oppose it. The words "the right way to play the game" won't be found on my lips. If a team wants to pursue a strategy that is within the rules and it works, then by all means, they have my blessing (not that they need it). Instead, my concern with The Shift is a worry that it doesn't work, or at least that it has a flaw that needs fixing.

The data show that while The Shift does a decent job of preventing singles on balls in play (what it's supposed to do), it also increases the number of walks that happen in front of it, and the number of additional walks outweighs the number of singles saved. It's a problem because you can't throw a guy out if he gets to walk to first base.

But the "why" was important. It seemed that The Shift was changing the way in which pitchers pitched. We saw that there were fewer fastballs thrown in front of The Shift than we might otherwise expect, and that pitchers tended to stay out of the strike zone a little more. Not by a lot. In fact, it might not even be visible to the naked eye. The percentage of pitches that are out of the zone goes from 51.0 to 53.3 from a standard defense (two right/two left) to a full shift (three on one side). That difference stands up even after we control for the types of hitters that get shifted against. And it's enough to drive up the walk rate to where it cancels out the benefits that teams thought they were getting with The Shift... and then some.

But there was some hope. I found that when individual pitchers stayed closer to the in-zone/out-of-zone mix that they used without The Shift on, they could still get the benefits of The Shift without the walk problems. So, in theory, a team could simply figure out a way to convince its pitchers to not fall prey to the walk trap and The Shift would once again be their friend.

It's reasonable to think that some teams might be more hip to this idea than others. Maybe some figured it out a year before the others. Maybe they were better at getting the message across to their pitchers. Or, maybe no one has figured it out yet.

Warning! Gory Mathematical Details Ahead!

I used data from 2015-2017, made available through MLB's data portal, Baseball Savant. They are kind enough to note when teams are using an infield shift (three fielders on one side of second base), as opposed to a "strategic shift" (someone's playing a bit out of position, but it's not quite that drastic) or a "standard" alignment.

Since we're doing this by team, I can't just look at raw walk rates, because we know that some teams have good pitchers and others have not-so-good pitchers. Some have a mix of both. I used the log-odds ratio method to take into account a batter's general walking proclivities, and a pitcher's as well, and then shoving them into a binary logistic regression. Then, I asked the computer to generate a specific coefficient for each team's pitchers, for when they went into The Shift and how that affected their walk rate.

Using those coefficients, I was able to project what would happen if a league-average pitcher faced a league-average hitter (which we expect would product a league-average walk rate; from 2015-2017, 7.7 percent of plate appearances ended in a walk) and then just switched his hat. Here's the top five and the bottom five:

Top 5 Teams	Projected Shift Walk Rate	Bottom 5 Teams	Projected Shift Walk Rate
Rockies	6.2%	Rangers	11.2%
Pirates	6.7%	Mets	10.4%
Indians	7.2%	Dodgers	10.2%
Astros	7.3%	Cardinals	9.9%
Braves	7.7%	Tigers	9.7%

There are probably people out there right now trying to figure out what the common thread is among the top and bottom teams. I'm sure, because this is Baseball Prospectus, people are already trying to make the case that sabermetric "early adopters" have some sort of edge here. I think that the more interesting piece is that by the time you get to fifth place in The Shift, we're at league average.

As a sanity check, I examined the issue on a pitch-by-pitch level, looking at how often pitchers threw their pitches in the GameDay strike zone, and again using the same basic methodology and getting team-specific coefficients. The names on the list re-arranged themselves, but the idea was the same, and the two lists correlated with an R of .593.

There's a reason that I don't usually do this type of leaderboard post. I don't really know what the Rockies, Pirates, Indians, Astros, and Braves have in common, or what they have that the bottom five don't. I can put a shrug emoji here and say, "Well, it must be something!" but that seems like a cop-out. Instead, I'd like to present another table and suggest that the table above doesn't even really matter anymore.

Year	League Percent Outside K Zone (Full Shift)	League Percent in K Zone (No Shift)	Difference
2015	54.1%	51.1%	3.0%
2016	53.3%	50.9%	2.4%
2017	52.6%	50.9%	1.7%
2018	52.0%	50.7%	1.3%

The hole in The Shift is fixing itself, and it's coming down really fast league wide. In my earlier work on The Shift, I suggested that until teams stopped having such a huge difference between their out-of-zone rate with and without The Shift on, there would just be too many walks for The Shift to make sense. It seems that all 30 of them have been working toward just that. I once estimated that it takes about 10 years for an idea to filter its way through baseball. At this rate, it looks like teams are going to catch up a lot faster than that. And yeah, they're all saber-smart now.

It's likely that whatever magic it was that the Rockies and Pirates had has made its way to Texas and Queens. Or is at least on its way. And if teams are committing to fixing the walk problem, then it's likely that they will continue shifting and shifting a lot.

And eventually it's going to actually make sense for them to do it.

—Russell Carleton is a former author of Baseball Prospectus and now an analyst for the New York Mets.

The State of the Quality Start

Rob Mains

One of the seven things you (probably) didn't know about the 2018 season is that quality starts—defined as a start lasting six or more innings with three or fewer earned runs allowed—as a percentage of total starts cratered to an all-time low of 41 percent. I want to look a little more deeply into this, since it's been a while (May of 2016, to be exact) since I've examined quality starts.

The term *quality start* is credited to *Philadelphia Inquirer* sportswriter John Lowe. It's been derided ever since he coined it in December of 1985. Three runs in six innings? That's a 4.50 ERA! In what world is that a measure of quality?

Let's start with that criticism. It's true that 3 x 9 / 6 = 4.5. (You came here for this sort of high-level math, right?) But it's also true that type of start, meeting the bare minimum for earning a quality start, is unusual. Here's the proportion of quality starts in which the pitcher lasted exactly six innings and yielded exactly three earned runs. (I'm going to confine this analysis to the 30-team era, 1998-present. Almost all data retrieved in this article is via the Baseball-Reference Play Index.)

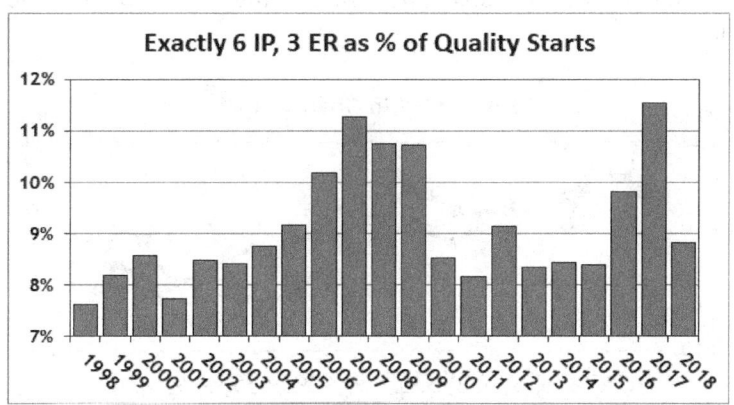

There were 1,997 quality starts in 2018. Only 176, or fewer than one in 11, featured a pitcher going six innings and allowing three earned runs. Put another way, the percentage of quality starts that resulted in a 4.50 ERA (8.8 percent) is less than half the percentage of games in which a batter hit two home runs and his team lost (22.5 percent; 237-69 won-lost). That doesn't impugn hitting two homers.

So if a 4.50 ERA isn't the norm, what is? How good are quality starts?

Pretty good, it turns out. First, on a team level:

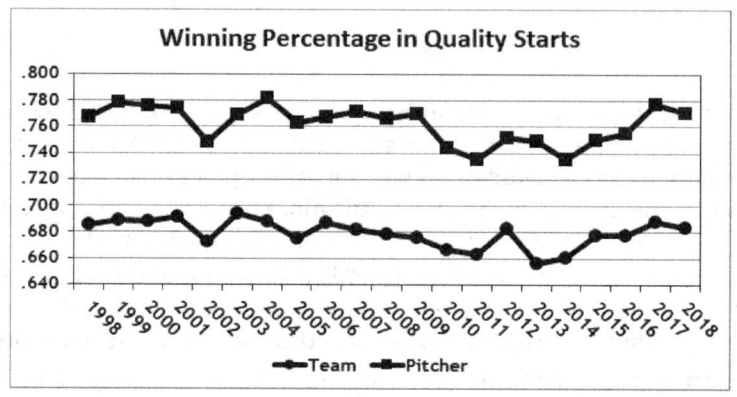

Teams receiving a quality start from their pitcher won 68.4 percent of their games in 2018, in line with the 30-team era average of 67.9 percent. A team with a .684 winning percentage wins 111 games. Getting a quality start is definitely a good thing. Individual pitchers throwing quality starts have a higher winning percentage because a big slice of team losses is assigned to a reliever.

If teams do well in quality starts, how well do the starting pitchers do? Again, very well.

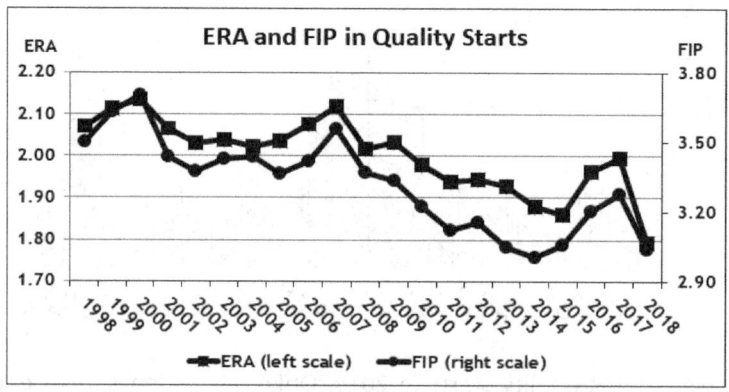

Pitchers in quality starts had a 1.79 ERA (blue line) in 2018, *the lowest in the 30-team era*. Their FIP was higher, 3.04, but still excellent. In the 30-team era, only 2014 had a lower FIP for quality starts, 3.01.

But, of course, the run environment in 2014 was different. Teams in 2014 scored 4.07 runs per game, the fewest in a non-strike year since 1976. They scored 4.45 runs per game in 2018. So surrendering a 3.04 FIP in 2018 is more impressive than 3.01 in 2014. Accordingly, let's look at ERA and FIP in quality starts relative to league averages.

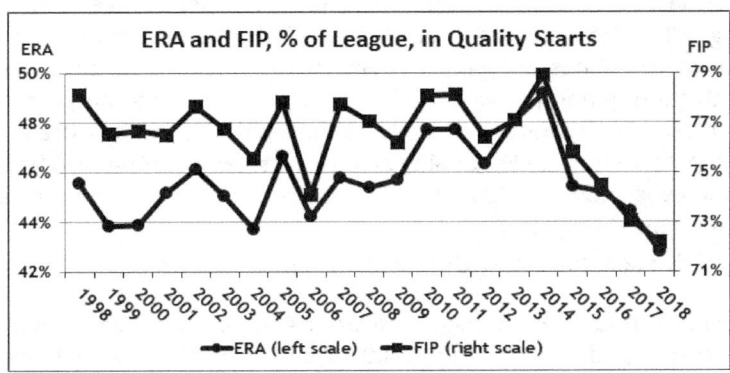

This tells a more dramatic story. Starting pitchers in 2018 gave up a 4.19 ERA and a 4.21 FIP. Starters in quality starts gave up a 1.79 ERA, 43 percent of the league average. Starters in quality starts gave up a 3.04 FIP, 72 percent of the league average. Both of these marks represent lows in the 30-team era.

The takeaway here is this: *Quality starts are better, relative to other starts, than they've ever been over the past 21 years.*

Maybe during the winter I'll look at this over a longer arc of time. For now, though, we can definitively say quality starts are the best they've ever been since the Diamondbacks and Rays joined the majors.

Yet, paradoxically, they're down.

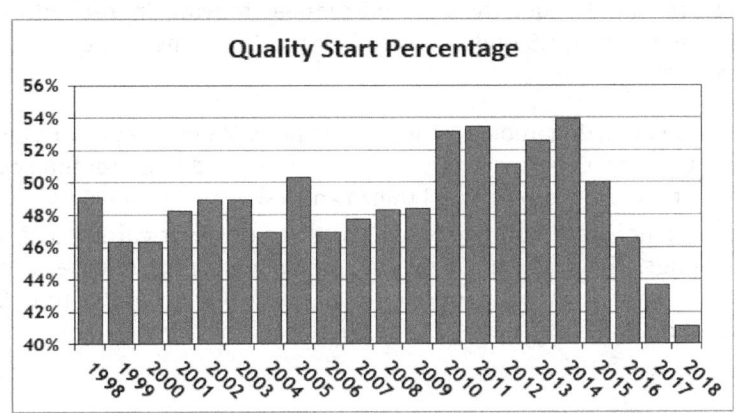

This graph covers only the 30-team era. In my article last week, though, I looked at the years 1908-2018. The result was the same. The 41 percent of starts in 2018 that were quality starts are an all-time low, well below the runners-up: 1930's 43 percent (the year teams scored an all-time record 5.55 runs per game) and last year's 44 percent.

The normal explanation for a dip in quality start percentage is an increase in scoring. When teams score a lot of runs, it's harder for starting pitchers to last six or more innings and limit opponents to three earned runs. From 1998 to 2014, the correlation between runs scored per game and the percentage of starts that were quality starts was -0.94. That means there was an extremely close relationship: More runs, fewer quality starts. Too small a sample? Go back to the start of the Expansion Era, 1961, and the relationship is even more negative, a -0.95 correlation, though 2014.

But that's broken down over the past four years:

- 2015: Runs per game increased from 4.07 to 4.25, quality start percentage decreased from 54.0 to 50.1. Yes, that's a negative relationship, but the regression model would predict a decline of 1.5 percentage points. We got 3.9 instead.
- 2016: Runs per game increased from 4.25 to 4.48, quality start percentage decreased from 50.1 to 46.6. Past experience would suggest a decline of just 1.8 percentage points. We got 3.4.
- 2017: Runs per game increased from 4.48 to 4.65, quality start percentage decreased from 46.6 to 43.6. Again, the direction's right, but the magnitude isn't. Using the relationship from 1998 to 2014, that increase in scoring should've reduced quality starts by 1.3 percentage points, not 2.9.
- 2018: Runs per game declined from 4.65 to 4.45. That should've resulted in the quality start percentage moving in the other direction, rising 1.6 points. It didn't. It fell 2.6 points, as noted, to an all-time low.

Granted, we're talking about just four years here. Maybe they're outliers. But I don't think they are. Quality starts, as noted, are as good or better than ever. But they're rarer than ever as well. And I think I know why.

To get a quality start, you need to allow three or fewer earned and pitch at least six innings. That's 18 outs. Here's a graph showing the number of starting pitchers who limited their opponents to three or fewer earned runs but got pulled after pitching at least five innings but fewer than six:

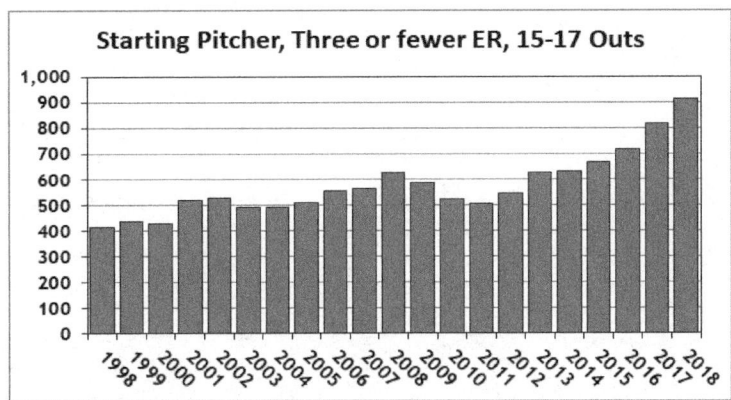

A pitcher getting 15 outs pitched five innings. A pitcher getting 16 outs pitched 5 1/3. A pitcher getting 17 outs pitched 5 2/3. More than ever before, pitchers are being removed from games in which they are within 1-3 outs of a quality start, falling just short of the six-inning finish line. Widespread acknowledgement of the times-through-the-order penalty and a flotilla of available bullpen arms is making the quality start simultaneously both more excellent and more rare.

Which is ironic, given that we saw a new post-war quality start record this season:

Rank	Pitcher	Season	Consecutive QS
1	Jacob deGrom	2018	24
2	Bob Gibson	1968	22
-	Chris Carpenter	2005	22
4	Johan Santana	2004	21
5	Luis Tiant	1968	20
-	Mike Scott	1986	20
-	Jake Arrieta	2015	20
8	Robin Roberts	1952	19
-	Tom Seaver	1973	19
-	Jack Morris	1983	19
-	Greg Maddux	1998	19
-	Josh Johnson	2010	19
-	Jon Lester	2014	19

While there have been longer streaks spread over multiple seasons, no pitcher since World War II threw more consecutive quality starts in one year than Jacob deGrom this year. The fact that he did in a year in which quality starts were the rarest they've ever been adds to the accomplishment.

—*Rob Mains is an author of Baseball Prospectus.*

Heads-Up Hacking—The First Pitch

Matthew Trueblood

Batters fell behind in a higher percentage of all plate appearances in 2018 than in any previous season for which we have pitch-by-pitch data. That kind of granular information goes back only to 1988, but we might safely assume (given all we know about baseball as it had been before that, and as it has been in the years since) that batters have *never* fallen behind at a higher rate than they did last season.

Through the 1990s, the percentage of all plate appearances that began 0-1 hovered in the high 30s and low 40s. In the 2000s, it rose steadily but slowly, through the mid-40s. In 2018, 49.8 percent of all trips to the plate began 0-1. That, as much as anything, captures in microcosm the nature of hitting in MLB today.

A countdown clock toward strike three begins ticking almost the moment a batter takes his place in the box. The league's adjusted OPS+ on the first pitch was higher in 2018 than ever before, and that has been true in most of the last 10 seasons. Batters hit .264/.289/.442 in all plate appearances in which they swung at the first pitch last season, and .241/.330/.395 in all plate appearances in which they took that first offering.

The percentage differences in batting average and isolated power there favor swinging at the first pitch by more than in any season since 1988, while the difference in on-base percentage favors taking by more than ever. If you want to get on base at a decent clip, it's a good idea to be patient, but you run the risk of missing the only chances you'll get to produce power.

Cleveland Indians 2019

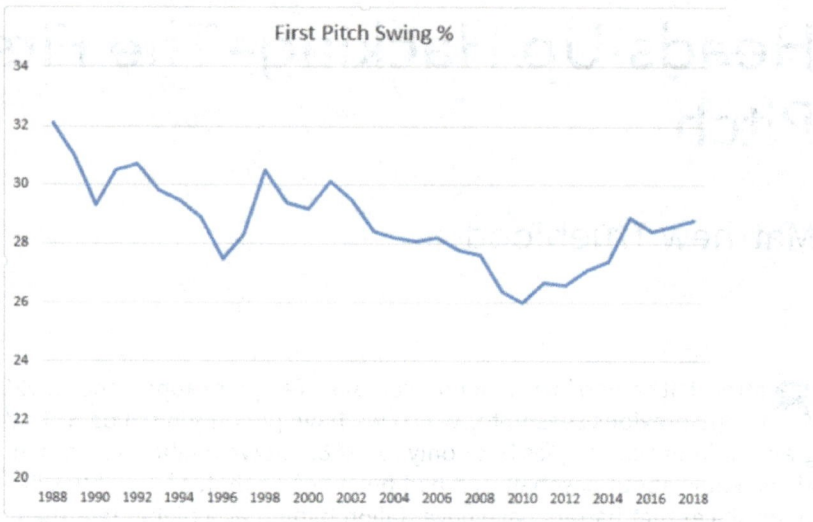

The league swung at the first pitch 28.8 percent of the time in 2018. With the isolated exception of 2015, that's the highest that number has climbed since 2002, but it might not be high enough. With the help of BP research maven Rob McQuown, I looked at the aggregate Called Strike Probability (CSProb) on the first pitch for each season since 2008, when the implementation of PITCHf/x first made measuring that possible. It's risen sharply during that period.

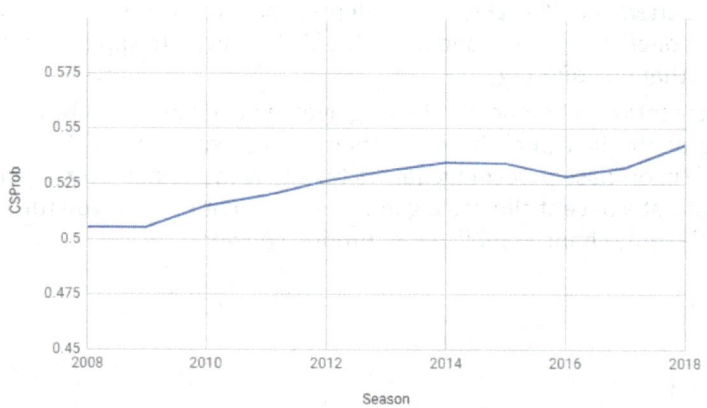

Called Strike Probability, First Pitch of PA (2008-2018)

Called Strike Probability is exactly what it sounds like: a pitch with a given CSProb has roughly that chance of being called a strike, if not swung at. In 2018, a batter who took 100 first pitches from a random sampling of the league's pitchers might expect to fall behind 54 or 55 times—up from 50 or 51 times in 2008. Almost regardless of pitch type (and, notably, especially in the case of fastballs), the first pitch tends to have more of the zone right now than ever before.

Pitchers are better at throwing strikes. They have better stuff, and believe more in their ability to miss bats within the zone. Perhaps most importantly, they know that batters are looking for one thing on the first pitch: a fastball. If they don't get it, they're likely to take the pitch. Check out how the use of sinkers and four-seamers on the first pitch has changed in a decade:

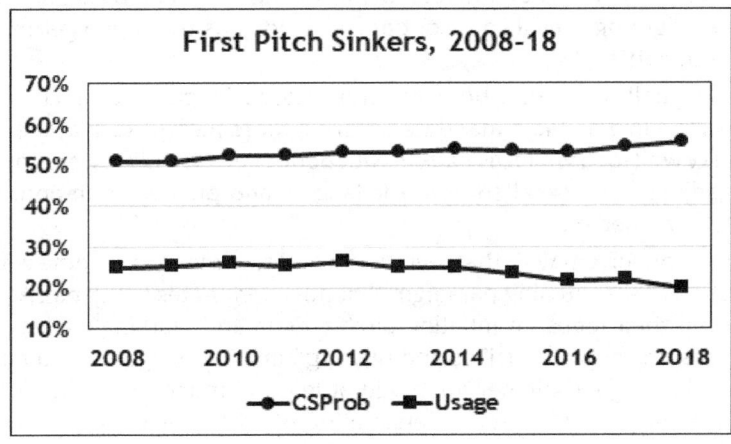

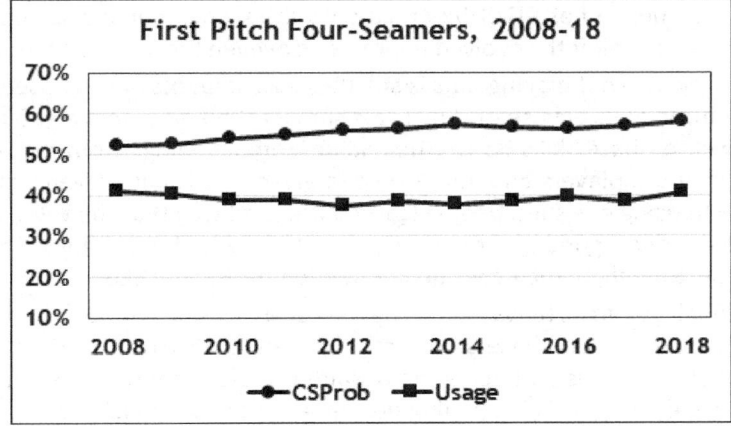

The sinker is losing its place in baseball, but the rate at which pitchers have thrown it on the first pitch hasn't dropped any faster than its usage rate in other counts. Pitchers have actually gone to their four-seamer *more* often to open counts, in the last few years, after a dip in the 2012-2015 period. What's really changed, though, and what shows up in both charts above, is that pitchers are catching more of the zone with first-pitch fastballs than they were a decade ago, or a half-decade ago. They're attacking right away, even with the pitch they know batters are expecting. The message is pretty clear: batters are being too passive.

Sliders, curves, and changeups each have more of the zone when thrown on the first pitch than they did several years ago, too, though the effect is less pronounced. Pitchers have seen the numbers; they know batters are doing better on the first pitch itself. They still feel safe throwing more and better strikes than ever before, figuring they'll come out ahead as long as they keep getting ahead to open each battle.

The Moneyball revolution brought an increased league-wide focus on OBP, which resulted in a de facto mandate to take a more patient tack at the plate. It worked very well for a while, as batters with poor plate discipline were compelled to either adjust or be expelled from the league, and pitchers with poor control were slowly weeded out.

However, concurrent with that revolution, and spurred by it in some ways, was the evolution of the pitching paradigm that now dominates the game. As batters ratcheted up their focus on inflating pitch counts and working walks, pitchers honed theirs on throwing strikes and missing bats. The league's understanding of what makes a good pitcher improved at least as much, from the mid-1990s through the mid-2000s, as its understanding of what makes a good hitter. As amphetamines and other performance-enhancing drugs were phased mostly out of the game, and as PITCHf/x broke onto the scene, individuals and teams learned how to exploit the evolved approaches of even the smartest hitters.

The ability to avoid making outs is still the most valuable one in baseball, but the magnitude of its eclipse of slugging is smaller than ever. To a greater extent than power, on-base skills derive their value from chaining—from the on-base skill levels of the players on either side of a given individual. Eleven years ago, when the housing crisis hit, people learned the hard way that the value of their homes depended a good deal on the values of their neighbors' homes. The same wasn't true, though, of their cars. So it is now, with OBP and SLG.

The global OBP in 2018 was .318. The only seasons since the Dead Ball Era in which the league got on base at a worse clip were 2013-2015, 1988, 1971-1972, and 1963-1968. This is all happening despite the aforementioned evolution of the science of hitting. It's happening despite a shift in approach and focus, one that would steer OBP ever higher, if only it were working.

Instead, it's sitting at a low ebb, and while it does so, even guys who get on base often are a little less helpful than they were 10 years ago—or 20, or 40, or 60, or 70, or 80, or 90. They're less helpful, that is, because unless there happen to be three or four other guys in the lineup who get on just as regularly, their contribution is merely to forestall the inevitable. Runs happen, increasingly, when a sudden bang happens, and that means attacking early in the count—because pitchers are sure as hell doing that.

In a league making contact on barely 75 percent of its swings, and a league in which an increasing number of pitchers can throw multiple off-speed pitches for strikes in any count, the only way to consistently generate offense is going to be aggressive. This isn't necessarily true for individuals, like Mookie Betts and Jose Ramirez, who make a lot of contact and have excellent plate discipline, and whose power comes from such natural quickness in a short stroke. Most players have to make tradeoffs, though, whether it be lowering their contact rate or raising their chase rate, in order to consistently make the quality of contact necessary to survive in today's game.

Highest %	Lowest %
Javier Baez – 48.3	Joe Mauer – 4.6
Freddie Freeman – 47.1	Mookie Betts – 9.7
Ozzie Albies – 46.3	Brett Gardner – 10.7
Jose Altuve – 44.2	Jose Ramirez – 12.0
Nick Castellanos – 44.1	Jason Kipnis – 13.8
Joey Gallo – 42.3	Jesus Aguilar – 14.5
Corey Dickerson – 40.9	Xander Bogaerts – 15.8
Salvador Perez – 40.8	Brian Dozier – 16.3
Eddie Rosario – 40.7	Mike Trout – 17.6
Nick Ahmed – 40.4	Yasmani Grandal – 17.6

Top 10 and Bottom 10 Hitters, First-Pitch Swing Rate (2018)

The question isn't which of these lists one prefers, but what they each convey, qualitatively, about the cat-and-mouse game of early-count hitting. Those top five on the left, especially, drive home the fact that for most players, getting aggressive early in the count is now key to keeping strikeout rate down and hitting for power.

For now, the message is: pitchers are coming right after batters with the nastiest stuff they've ever had. Batters had better stop giving away strike one and force hurlers to adjust, or the global OBP crisis is only going to get worse.

—*Matthew Trueblood is an author of Baseball Prospectus.*

A Hymn for the Index Stat

Patrick Dubuque

We survived without computers. I know this, because I remember the day when my dad hooked up his brand-new Atari 400 computer to the back of our 12-inch Magnavox television, and the perfect blue of the memo pad lit up for the first time. I was born just on the edge of that transitional generation, of learning cursive and balancing checkbooks and just doing math all the time, constant manual arithmetic.

It still amazes me. We learned how to sail ships without computers. We learned how to do calculus. We built towers that didn't fall down, most of the time. We engineered catapults to knock them down anyway. We built a robust system of philosophy called "utilitarianism," founded on the principle that the good of an action is evaluated by summing the effects of that action, which is the kind of formula that would make the world's mainframes crash. The whole foundation of statistics as a field is "here's math you could easily do but would die of old age first."

The fact of the matter is that there is too much math in the world to do. There are too many things changing, and too many things too small to notice, for us to handle. At some point, they become too much for the computers to handle as well, which is why we have chaos theory and undetectable earthquakes, but it's not an even fight. At some point, we fall back on intuition, and given how under-equipped we are, we're forced to bestow that intuition with some sort of supernatural superiority, the "gut feeling," that we can't prove because we can only intuit that our intuition is better.

We're all lousy at intuition, and wonderful at lying to ourselves about it. The honest truth is that computers are far better at intuition than we are, because in order to know what feels "off" you have to know what's "on." In order to do that you have to constantly reassess the average of everything, then re-rank your own experience against it.

Test your own, by comparing these three anonymous lines:

Player	G	HR	AVG	OBP	SLG
Player A	156	38	.259	.342	.535
Player B	154	38	.280	.348	.527
Player C	158	38	.266	.343	.509

These all seem like pretty similar players, right? The second one a touch more batted-ball dependent, the third a little less strong, but all pretty good hitters. And you'd be right, about the latter. Not the former.

Here's the breakdown:

- Player A: 1991 Howard Johnson, 141 DRC+
- Player B: 1996 Dean Palmer, 121 DRC+
- Player C: 2018 Giancarlo Stanton, 114 DRC+

Baseball is fortunate to have escaped the seismic shifts of so many other sports, where the talents and performances of other eras are nearly unrecognizable. (And not just other sports: try to explain the greatness of the movie Duck Soup without adjusting for era.) But they're still there, and they're nearly impossible to account for manually, without having to resort to sweeping generalizations like "steroid era" or juiced-ball era" to throw out entire swathes of production.

This is all to say that we should celebrate the index stat, that simple 100-based scale with such a humble aim: just to give context. It's hard to imagine how we lived without them for so long. Sabermetricians have always tried to make their stats look like other stats: True Average mapped to batting average, FIP molded to look like and compare to ERA. It's easy to understand the motivation—these statistics carry an emotional value in them that is hard to resist, as with the .300 hitter and the 2.00 ERA—but even they fall prey to the same loss of scale as their unadjusted counterparts. If a .300 average means different things in different years, does that hold true for a .300 True Average?

Instead, 100 doesn't say anything, except above average or below. And it does it instantly, for every season in every run environment for any statistic we want it to. We should have more index stats: K%+, so we can stop comparing Mike Clevinger's career 9.46 K/9 to Nolan Ryan's 9.55. HBP%+, so we can note that Ron Hunt was getting plunked when nobody else was getting plunked, as opposed to that imitator Brandon Guyer. Some might note how stale these references are and accuse league-adjustment as a backward-looking drive, and this is true. But we're always looking backward, always comparing the new with the expectations already set. The index stat just forces us to be honest.

There's always resistance to a new statistic, especially one so outwardly simple and so internally complex. We tend to stick with what we know, even in the case of formulas that are supposed to tell us what we know. But if your resistance is that it seems too complicated, too counterintuitive, too "black boxy," I encourage you to consider why you feel that way. Because the real world is infinitely more complicated than baseball, where all the pitches go in one basic direction and the baserunners are only allowed to travel in four directions. Baseball statistics based on mixed methodology are almost impossibly intricate. So are skyscrapers and automobiles. That's why we have computers—to take the guesswork out of them.

—*Patrick Dubuque is an author of Baseball Prospectus.*

Index of Names

Allen, Greg 22
Barnes, Brandon 93
Bauer, Trevor 52
Bauers, Jake 24
Benson, Will 81, 106
Bieber, Shane 54
Bradley, Bobby 82, 106
Carrasco, Carlos 56
Carter, Jodd 93
Chang, Yu-Cheng 83, 102
Cimber, Adam 95
Civale, Aaron 89
Clevinger, Mike 58
Clippard, Tyler 60
Cole, A.J. 62
Collins, Gavin 93
Delgado, Raynel 93
Edwards, Jon 95
Federowicz, Tim 93
Flaherty, Ryan 26
Freeman, Mike 93
Freeman, Tyler 84
Goody, Nick 95
Grimm, Justin 95
Haase, Eric 93, 107
Hand, Brad 64
Hankins, Ethan 90, 103
Hentges, Sam 95, 102
Hillman, Juan 95
Hoyt, James 95
Hu, Chih-Wei 66
Ice, Logan 93
Johnson, Daniel 85
Jones, Nolan 86, 101
Joyce, Matt 28
Karinchak, James 106
Kipnis, Jason 30
Kluber, Corey 68
Lindor, Francisco 32
Luplow, Jordan 34
Martin, Leonys 36
McKenzie, Triston 91, 99
Mercado, Oscar 87
Moroff, Max 93
Naquin, Tyler 38
Naylor, Bo 88, 104
Olson, Tyler 70
Otero, Dan 72
Oviedo, Luis 95, 100
Papi, Mike 93
Perez, Oliver 74
Perez, Roberto 40
Plawecki, Kevin 42
Plutko, Adam 95
Ramirez, Hanley 44
Ramirez, Jose 46
Ramirez, Neil 76
Rocchio, Brayan 93, 105
Rodriguez, Jefry 95
Salazar, Danny 92
Sandlin, Nick 95, 105
Santana, Carlos 48

Stamets, Eric 93
Taylor, Ben 95
Torres, Lenny 95, 103
Valera, George 100
Wilson, Alex 79
Wittgren, Nick 95
Zimmer, Bradley 50

Ballpark diagrams for Baseball Prospectus are created by THIRTY81Project, a design concept offering original ballpark artwork, including the new 'Ballparks of 2019' 11 x 17 color print.

Visit **www.thirty81project.com** for full details.